Two of a Kind

TWO of a KIND

The **Morecambe and Wise** *Story*

Paul Burton

First published in 2020 by Fantom Publishing, an imprint of Fantom Films
www.fantompublishing.co.uk

A catalogue record for this book is available from the British Library.

Hardback edition ISBN: 978-1-78196-337-1

Typeset by Phil Reynolds Media Services, Leamington Spa
Printed and bound by CPI Group (UK) Ltd, Croydon, CR0 4YY

Jacket front photo: ITV/Shutterstock

This book is dedicated to the memory of Eric Morecambe and Ernie Wise.

Contents

WHEN MORECAMBE AND WISE were at the height of their fame and success there was no doubt in my mind that this was a fifty/fifty partnership. They were both as good as each other and had an equal part to play in one of the best and funniest double acts that has ever graced the entertainment business in this country.

– Bill Cotton

Foreword

IN 1965, I WAS lucky enough to be cast in the role of Claudette on Morecambe and Wise's second feature film for Rank, which was called *That Riviera Touch*. Knowing that I would be working with England's number one comedy double act made me wonder if they would have big egos. But in this case, their egos were left outside the studio gates. Eric and Ernie were two professionals who were dedicated to making people laugh.

Comedy can be a serious business. Both men were concerned that their natural spontaneity would suffer under the continual demands of repeated 'takes' caused by the suppressed giggles from the cast, crew and visitors alike – not to mention the time it took to make the various camera, lighting and sound changes! At first, I found myself watching Eric and Ernie like an audience member, but I quickly pulled myself together and gave them what they expected from me – my character, Claudette.

The boys deserve to be the subject of this new biography. They were delicious and delightful to work with. Pensive when the cameras weren't rolling, professional and focused when they were. Eric was thoughtful and concerned for others; Ernie bubbled with an inner sense of fun. They complemented one another.

I hope you enjoy reading this book.

Suzanne Lloyd
March 2020

Introduction

MORECAMBE AND WISE'S BRILLIANCE as performers, which brought pleasure to millions of people during their careers, was shaped throughout a long journey. They paid their dues and only reached the top through a combination of talent, persistence and sheer hard work. Given what they went on to achieve, it's strange to think that there was a time, before Morecambe and Wise became successful, when Ernie was disillusioned with the double act. Indeed, he even sent a letter to Eric expressing how he felt:

Dear Eric,

Thanks for your letter. Well Eric I want to come straight to the point. I want us to break up the act. I'm afraid it won't work. I have such a terrific amount of animosity to put up with at home. I feel it would be better if we parted. I know this will be quite a shock for you, but I had to come to some sort of decision. I can't go on as things are, I'm not satisfied with my work, I have lost a lot of zip and it will take time to regain it. I can't keep you waiting around for me, I don't know definitely when I will be out. I feel it's a great pity after we had planned so much, but my mind's made up.

He ended the letter by saying:

All I know is that I want us to remain friends. Hoping to hear from you.
>Your best pal,
>Ernie

Frustratingly, it is not possible to put an exact date on the letter, which Eric kept. What is known, however, is that Morecambe responded immediately saying he'd never heard such rubbish and that Ernie should have a few days' rest and then they'd get back to finding some work. Thankfully, this is what duly happened.

In this book, I have, as you would expect, written Eric and Ernie's story. At the same time, I have also made every effort to shine a spotlight on lesser known parts of their lives and careers.

There are several people I would like to thank for their help and support while I have been writing and researching this publication. Firstly, my special thanks go to Suzanne Lloyd for writing the foreword. A debt of gratitude is also due to the following people for sharing their recollections with me: Bobby Ball, Lionel Blair, Ted Childs, Jan Clennell, Susan Colclough, Jim Davidson, Michele Dotrice, Tom Edwards, Hannah Gordon, Michael Grade, Ann Hamilton, Tony Hare, Tony Hatch, Eddie Izzard, Diane Keen, Patricia Ward Kelly, Ronnie Le Drew, Janet Mahoney, Leigh Miles, Zoe Nicholas, Valerie Van Ost, Nick Owen, Simon Pegg, Denise Rayner, Carol Royle, Pamela Salem, David Schulten, Madeline Smith, Richard Stone, Jimmy Tarbuck, Ian Thom, Mike Vardy, Roger Wash, Denise Waterman, Peter Willcocks and Mike Yarwood. I shall also be forever grateful to the late Bruce Forsyth, Ray Galton and Alan Simpson, Dennis Kirkland and Vince Powell for sharing their Morecambe and Wise related thoughts with me in the latter parts of their careers.

For their invaluable assistance, I am indebted to Jane Foster and Alexandra Henwood at FremantleMedia for helping with my archive requests relating to Morecambe and Wise's years at Thames Television. I would also like to sincerely thank Ian Freeman for putting me in contact with Michael Grade. Furthermore, I am extremely grateful to Louis Barfe for his kind help when I was researching Johnny Ammonds' and Ernest Maxin's working relationships with Morecambe and Wise.

I would also like to take this opportunity to send my best wishes to the Morecambe family, whom I am proud to know.

I sincerely hope you will find this new biography about Morecambe and Wise both entertaining and informative.

Paul Burton
March 2020

1
In the Beginning

ALTHOUGH MORECAMBE CAME BEFORE Wise in the name of their double act, Ernie Wise (real name: Ernest Wiseman) was born before Eric, in St James' Hospital in Leeds on 27 November 1925 to parents Harry and Connie Wiseman. Strangely, his birthday was not registered until January 1926. At the time of his birth, Ernie's parents were living in a single room at 6 Atlanta Street in Bramley, Leeds. He was their eldest child and was followed by Gordon, Ann, Constance and Arthur. Sadly, Arthur died from peritonitis, the inflammation of the thin layer of tissue called the peritoneum that lines the inside of the abdomen, when he was just two years old.

Harry's main occupation saw him employed on the railways. He worked his way up from being a signal and light man to a railway porter. Connie, meanwhile, was once a box-loom operator in Pudsey, earning three pounds a week. Although Harry's family approved of the pairing, resulting from a meeting on a tram, Connie's family cut her off without a penny after she defied her mill-owner father and went ahead with her wedding to Harry in 1924.

Despite the ill treatment Connie received, the Wiseman family later made intermittent visits to the New Inn, a pub her father ran in Farsley near Pudsey following his retirement. Nonetheless, her father never changed his opinion of his son-in-law. When her father died, Connie remained excluded as a beneficiary from the will and it was her siblings – Nellie and Annie – who were given her share.

When the Wiseman family left Atlanta Street, Ernie found himself living at 35 Warder Street, Bramley, Leeds, just four miles away from his first home. The family would remain here for five years. A twenty-mile journey then relocated them to 29 Tombridge Crescent, Kinsley, near Hemsworth, West Yorkshire, in October 1931. The Wisemans also stayed there for a period of five years before moving to 12 Station Terrace, Ardsley, between Wakefield and Leeds, and not far from Ardsley Station.

Although of no great significance, Ernie never forgot his two earliest memories. The first consisted of someone driving a limousine down the street, and of him somehow managing to take a ride in the back of the car. The second involved a lady having a motor-cycling accident and Ernie's father, who was in the St John Ambulance, attending to her injured knee.

Eric Morecambe (real name: John Eric Bartholomew) was born in Morecambe, Lancashire, on 14 May 1926 at 12.30pm to parents George and Sadie Bartholomew. He was an only child. Although Eric was not born in hospital, which was nothing unusual for the time, he was not born in the family home either. In fact, he was born in the front room of 42 Buxton Street, Morecambe – his aunt's house. This was because his parents were having some repairs to their own house – number 48 – at the time.

Eric's father, George, worked for Morecambe Corporation, while his mother, Sadie, spent time working as a theatre usherette on the Central Pier in Morecambe. The couple met during a dance at the Winter Gardens in the resort. 'Sadie was a fascinating character,' remembered Eric's daughter, Gail. 'She was tiny, but she had a raucous laugh and a sharp tongue and would always call a spade a spade.'

It's strange to think that the world may have been deprived of the magic of Morecambe and Wise if the one-time planned emigration of Eric, his parents and uncle and auntie had taken place. As history thankfully proves, this did not happen.

Harry Wiseman was a talented performer who took to playing working men's clubs to supplement the family finances. Connie was also talented and played the piano, but did not perform in public due mainly to her shyness. Arguably, a busy family life also did little to make it possible for her to consider following her husband and eldest son onto the stage.

At the tender age of just six or seven, Ernie finally persuaded his mother to teach him a song. This led to the young boy performing 'The Sheikh of Araby' – a 1921 song that would later be recorded by Tommy Cooper – in front of his father at home one evening. Convinced that Ernie had talent, Harry and Connie proceeded to teach Ernie further song and dance routines. In time, Ernie joined forces with his father in a double act called Carson and Kid (sometimes known as Bert Carson and his Little Wonder and even The Two Tetleys, a tribute to a local alcoholic beverage) – the first of two double acts he would share the limelight with, albeit on different scales.

Harry and Ernie's performances at working men's clubs and pubs at weekends also helped with the family finances. Singing, crosstalk and even clog dancing all formed part of their act. 'The faster I danced, the faster the crowds threw money,' Ernie explained. Although essentially a double act, Harry and Ernie performed their own solo spots as well as performing together during the same shows. The close bond the father and son team had was further enhanced as their act became more and more popular in the clubs in the area. Ernie had caught the performing bug – a bug that would ultimately lead to bigger, better and more profitable opportunities in showbiz. Ernie's onscreen persona, developed later during the Morecambe and Wise years, may have seen him being careful with money, to an almost Scrooge-like degree; but his real-life upbringing and the struggles his family experienced meant that he remained cautious with his finances during his adult life. If there was money in the bank, he felt safe and secure.

Ernie's school years saw him attend Thorpe Infant and Junior School, and later East Ardsley Boys' School. However, he did not enjoy his school years, later admitting that he didn't really like the teachers or the authority they had over him. 'I've never really been a great learner,' Ernie would confess. 'I found it very hard to learn, even the dialogue for the shows – I have to really pound it in. Some people are marvellous. I can't, I have to work hard at learning anything.'

The education authority in Leeds was not as impressed by Ernie's sojourns into performing. The late nights were taking their toll. 'We didn't have the luxury of a motor car in those days,' remembered Ernie. 'We depended on the local buses. It didn't take us home, it always used to bring us near home about three or four miles away. My father used to carry me on his shoulders, and I'd be fast asleep as we'd get home about midnight. But I had to be in school on the Monday morning.' This often resulted in young Ernest falling asleep during lessons. This might not have been healthy or practical, but as the act was continuing to prove profitable, Harry ignored the education authority's concerns. Instead, he booked dates in working men's clubs and pubs out of the immediate area. Ernie never forgot how beneficial the extra money was. 'We used to earn three pounds fifty over the weekend,' he recalled. 'Which, of course, was more money than my father earned on the railway.'

Like Ernie, Eric never had any real interest in school. His school reports were lamentable. One of his headmasters even went as far as to say, 'This boy will never get anywhere in life.' Away from the confines of the normal school classroom, Eric was taken along to singing lessons and dancing classes. The latter were taken at Miss Hunter's dancing school in Morecambe.

To fund all the lessons, Sadie, in addition to her work as an usherette, worked part-time as a waitress. 'Sadie was completely extraordinary,' said Eric's daughter, Gail. 'If she'd been born now, she'd have been a very dynamic, successful, professional woman. She was very keen to help Dad get out of a very working-class life. She was incredibly aware that he was a one-off. She was clearly incredibly proud.'

Eric reminded an interviewer of one of the reasons why his mother was so keen for her son to succeed. 'It was all northern people's ambition in those days to get their youngsters onto the stage,' he pointed out. 'Because that's where the money was.'

The dance classes led Eric to performing in a song and dance act with a girl from the area called Molly Bunting – a name, one feels, that would not look out of place in a typical Morecambe and Wise sketch! Solo appearances were also the order of the day for Eric, who performed in clubs in his local area.

In 1936, Eric began piano lessons, amongst learning how to play other instruments. Thirty-seven years later, Eric and Ernie were interviewed by Valerie Singleton on the debut edition of the children's chat show, *Val Meets the VIPs*. Eric explained that he learned the piano, clarinet and trombone as a boy, but was not sufficiently proficient on any of the instruments. He did go on to point out, however, that even though his playing skills were basic, he had been able to use them within many of the sketches he and Ernie appeared in on their television shows – his example being playing the piano in the 'Grieg Piano Concerto' sketch.

As a child performer, Eric impersonated (on his own!) both members of the double act Flanagan and Allen. Comedy stars were always an inspiration to Eric. These included the uke-playing Lancashire comedian, George Formby. Arthur Askey would also earn Eric's heartfelt admiration, not least for his ability to ad-lib. Like Askey, Eric developed a very quick wit. By all accounts, it was a side of him that was always there, but this had a downside, as Eric once confided to the actress Hannah Gordon. 'I walk into a room and people expect me to be funny,' he said. This is something that the television executive Michael Grade once verified. 'If he had a crowd, Eric couldn't disappoint,' he explained. 'He liked the banter.' But Bruce Forsyth remembered that there were two sides to Eric when he was offstage. 'You could have a serious conversation with Eric,' he said. 'But as soon as a third person arrived then he would turn into Eric the comic!'

The year 1936 saw Ernie begin to make higher-profile appearances as a solo performer. His act consisted of him singing, dancing and telling jokes, dressed like a mini Charlie Chaplin in a bowler hat and a cut-down evening dress suit. The same year saw the Nignog Ring, a popular club launched by the *Northern Echo* news-paper in County Durham on 21 October 1929, enjoying popularity with the nation's youth. To put things into context, it should be made clear that Nig and Nog were

In the Beginning

two cartoon characters. To quote club publicity of the time, they were 'two little imps who live in the land of the moon, their chief occupation being to keep the Man in the Moon awake'. Amongst the club's other activities, a Nignog Troupe toured the various Rings with a gang show entitled, wait for it, *Nignogs Ahoy!* Due to the club's huge popularity amongst youngsters, other local newspapers introduced Nignog Rings. It was thanks to the *Bradford Telegraph and Argus*'s Nignog Troupe that Ernest Wiseman was able to make his debut on his biggest stage to date. The newspaper sponsored a charity revue staged at the Alhambra Theatre in Bradford. The title of the show would never find its way onto theatre hoardings now; back then, however, eyebrows weren't raised when the Alhambra proudly advertised the *Nignog Revue*, which ran for a week. In total, Ernie appeared in three of the annual Nignog revues between 1936 and 1938.

In 1938, Ernie, the boy who would later be billed as 'England's Mickey Rooney', took further tentative steps in 'the business called show' when he successfully auditioned for the impresario Bryan Michie at the Leeds Empire. Michie was a leading show-business impresario of the era who cast his variety shows with talented young performers he discovered during the auditions he held around the country. Although his audition would ultimately help Ernest on his way up the showbiz ladder, it would be the final nail in the coffin for the father and son act – something from which Harry Wiseman never recovered. That said, in the short term, at least, nothing changed. With no work being offered by the impresario, Ernie continued as if the audition had never happened. Save for the excitement of a paid radio broadcast of a talent competition he appeared in, it was business as usual.

Finally, opportunity came knocking again when Ernie was invited to audition for Jack Hylton in his London office. Hylton was a pianist, composer, band-leader and a colleague of Bryan Michie, which is how he came to hear about Ernest.

Taking a break from working as a porter on the railways, Harry accompanied his son on a train down to the capital on 6 January 1939. Ernie sang and danced for Hylton while Harry proudly watched on. Harry and Ernie then performed parts of the double act together for the impresario. The audition went so well that Ernie found himself being offered the opportunity to make his West End debut the same night in the stage version of the hugely popular radio series, *Band Waggon*.

To put into context just how much of a big deal Ernie's break was, one needs to know a little more about the history of *Band Waggon*. The radio series starred the popular comedian and actor Arthur Askey, best known for his catchphrase, 'Ay-Thang-Yew', and

Richard 'Stinker' Murdoch. Askey had been cast in the BBC radio version in 1938. It was the first comedy and variety radio series to be broadcast in Britain on the same day each week.

Although on the face of it the show had everything going for it, the early episodes did not exactly set the world on fire. The axe that hovered over the series was eventually lifted thanks to Askey, Murdoch and writer Vernon Harris. The three men reworked the programme and it very quickly caught listeners' imagination. At its peak, it was estimated that twenty million people listened to the series on the wireless.

The success of the radio show had inspired Jack Hylton to produce a stage version. Following a short tour, he moved the show to the Princes Theatre (now the Shaftesbury Theatre). Inexplicably, this wasn't proving to be popular. However, the arrival of Ernest Wiseman did bring a temporary boost to the show. The following article explains what happened next to the fledgling performer:

> Fresh oop fra' Yorkshire this week, a thirteen-year-old boy made a surprise debut on the London stage – his first professional appearance – in *Band Waggon* at the Princes' Theatre last night.
>
> His name is Ernest Wiseman, but, said Mr Jack Hylton, introducing him, 'he's going to be famous; so, we'll call him Ernie Wise'.

This 4ft-and-a-bit singer and dancer had not been announced to appear.

He came on without a sign of nerves, full of Yorkshire cockiness, sang – in a voice that made microphones unnecessary – 'I'm Knee-Deep in Daisies' and 'Let's Have a Tiddly at the Milk Bar', cracked a pair of North Country jokes, and did a whirlwind step dance, with terrific aplomb and efficiency.

Ernie is a sort of Yorkshire Max Miller, tilts his battered bowler over his eye, has a wicked wink.

He is the son of a railway porter from Ardsley, who taught him a few dance steps when he was three, and a mother who plays the piano.

Most of his astonishing technique was picked up from films and touring comedians.

Off stage he gives an even better performance. He has been in London only since Tuesday, but nothing daunts him.

Any brothers and sisters? 'Aye, two of each. They're all younger than me,' he grins, 'I'm the gaffer.'

'Who's looking after me?' He slaps his chest and winks. 'I can look after myself.'

He lives between Leeds and Wakefield. 'Isn't Wakefield the prison where they play cricket?' someone asked. 'Aye.' He comes back without hesitation. 'But warders always win!' But star or no star, he will have to go to school on Monday in London.

With Ernie's very proud father, Harry, choosing to return home to his wife and family, it was down to Jack

Hylton to ensure his new star signing was well looked after.

When the run at the Princes Theatre ended, *Band Waggon* was taken on another national tour. Despite the show not being a huge success in London initially, its popularity grew and eventually, the production, including Ernie, came back to the West End for a run at The London Palladium. This time the cast was joined by Tommy Trinder.

When the Second World War began, the government announced that all theatres were to close. Although the theatres quickly reopened, Jack Hylton had to abandon plans for more performances of *Band Waggon* for the foreseeable future. Ernie was invited to go and stay with Jack Hylton, his wife and children at their Sussex home.

Although he was made very welcome, Ernie later decided to make his way home. His parents had moved again and were now living at 17 Oxley Street, Pontefract Lane, Leeds. If Ernie had expected a hero's welcome, he was to be disappointed. The atmosphere was cool. Indeed, his parents couldn't understand why he had returned. With his father's health having deteriorated, and the family needing money, Ernie reluctantly took a job as a coalman's labourer.

In February 1940, Eric took part in a talent competition staged in Hoylake. The following extracts are from an article about the event printed in an issue of *Melody Maker* dated 2 March 1940:

> The Lancashire and Cheshire auditions of *The Melody Maker* talent search, in connection with Jack Hylton's radio and stage feature, *Youth Takes a Bow*, came to a thrilling climax at the Kingsway Cinema, Hoylake, last Saturday evening.
>
> Ten youthful entrants, who had succeeded in reaching the finals, appeared on the stage. From them, four have been selected to travel to London for their special auditions before compère Bryan Michie and Jack Hylton.

Later the article mentioned:

> The four to travel to London are Eric Bartholomew, of Morecambe, Anne Reynolds, Patricia Davey and Marion Perry. The three girls are all from Liverpool!
>
> Interviewed by a *Melody Maker* representative, Eric Bartholomew, who put over a brilliant comedian act, which caused the audience to roar with laughter, said, 'My ambition is to become a comedian. My hero is George Formby, another native of Lancashire. I would certainly like to follow in his footsteps.'

Although *Melody Maker* claims the audition took place in London, this is somewhat confusing as Eric himself pointed out a location in Manchester, where the audition took place, to his son Gary during a visit to the city. Maybe there were two auditions – or maybe the first audition was changed to Manchester? It's hard to tell. Either way, it was at this audition that Ernie saw Eric for the very first time. Eric's mother, Sadie, was also present.

By now, Ernie had returned to touring and was appearing in *Youth Takes a Bow* as a solo performer. The show featured more experienced adult performers in the first half, and younger less experienced performers in the second half. Decades later, Ernie could still clearly remember Eric's audition. 'He sang a song called "I'm Not All There",' Wise said. 'He had a beret and he wore a cut-down evening dress suit, like an Ascot suit, with a very big safety pin in the front. And he had a bootlace tie and held a big lollipop.' It was a song Eric later admitted he never enjoyed singing. The first venue at which Eric was paid to sing the song was the Jubilee Club in Morecambe. Indeed, it was also the first occasion he was paid to perform. Ernie watched Eric's audition for Hylton from the auditorium and realised that he had strong competition. Was Ernie jealous of how well Eric's audition had gone? No, but it's fair to say his confidence took a little knock.

Although it's been claimed that Eric and Ernie didn't meet at the audition, Eric's son, Gary, recalls his father saying otherwise. 'My father categorically stated he shared a few words with Ernie at the audition in Manchester. He thought Ernie was a bit of a big-head! Of course, it turned out that Ernie was only like that because he was worried that this boy from nowhere, whom Jack Hylton clearly liked, might depose him!'

Eventually, Eric received an invitation to join the company of *Youth Takes a Bow* as a solo performer while the show was playing at the Empire Theatre in Nottingham. Although they would eventually receive the same fees as a double act, back then the two boys were being paid different wages. This was due to Ernie's experience on the West End stage. It's probably fair to say that each of the boys was worried by the other's presence in the company. Eric was aware of Ernie's previous experience, and Ernie remembered the positive impression Eric had made at his audition. If there was any ill feeling or jealousy between the young performers, fate was about to intervene and bring Eric and Ernie closer together.

Bryan Michie, who was billed as 'Radio's Famous Compere', also acted as the compere of *Youth Takes a Bow*. The new performers in the cast were listed on the poster in the following order: Arthur Tolcher (who would later make numerous attempts to play the harmonica on *The Morecambe and Wise Show* before being told, 'Not now Arthur'), Helva Rintala, Ernie Wise, Mary Naylor, Dorothy Duval, Tommy Thompson, Jean

Bamford, Eddie Gunter, Frank Hines, Eric Bartholomew and Stan Vassie.

At the Swansea Empire, with his mother, Sadie, in tow, Eric was finally able to get properly acquainted with Ernie and vice versa. An incident later in the tour, in which Ernie was unable to find board and lodgings when they were playing the New Theatre in Oxford, saw Sadie come to his rescue. Amusingly, Eric and Ernie, out of necessity, ended up sharing a bed – something viewers would later see them do together in many a sketch on television! 'Sadie took a shine to Ernie immediately and booked accommodation wherever they went for both of them,' explained Eric's wife, Joan Morecambe. 'They didn't sort of hit it off right away because there was that little bit of competition between the two of them. But after then they became very big friends.' Sadie's proposal that Ernie should travel and stay with her and Eric, and that she should make all arrangements, was a relief for Ernie. He felt he had someone looking out for him again.

At this stage, Eric and Ernie were just like any other young lads forming a friendship in the workplace. Their job just happened to be performing, and their workplace just happened to be the number two variety theatres of this Sceptic Isle. Their friendship would always come first, though. Asked in a 1978 television interview how they had made their friendship last, Eric replied seriously, but with a dash of his trademark wit. 'Well, first of all, we like each other. I think that's important,' he said. 'It's a marriage with the laughs. He makes me laugh, and I think I make him laugh.'

It was while carrying out her official role as chaperone, and unofficial one as business manager, that Sadie suggested Eric and Ernie should form and work as a double act. This, she felt, would be more productive than just entertaining themselves on the train journey between Birmingham, where they were staying, and Coventry, where they were performing their solo acts. Once a four-minute act (including a song and dance routine and some typical jokes of the day) had been devised, Eric and Ernie were keen to test it on a paying audience. Sadie, too, felt they were ready; but it was only after Bryan Michie had seen the act, and Jack Hylton had suggested a change of song, that they would both give their blessing.

Finally, the premiere of Bartholomew and Wise's first double-act routine took place on Friday 28 August 1941 at the Empire Theatre, Liverpool (now called the Liverpool Empire). From now on, Eric and Ernie were more than just friends: they were business partners, a double act sharing the highs and lows that such an association brings and, importantly, the money it pays – good and bad. The act, which consisted of crosstalk that ended with a rendition of 'Only a Bird in a Gilded

Cage' and a soft-shoe shuffle, convinced Sadie, Jack and the audience that night that Eric and Ernie had a future as a double act. They had a long way to go, but the spark that made the act unique was already there – even in the act's infancy. Although Eric and Ernie would be required to keep to the contractual obligation of performing their respective solo acts, wherever possible they would be allowed to continue to perform their double act.

The first joke that Eric and Ernie performed on stage was a simple one. Eric used to run onto the stage with a chair and a long fishing line with an apple on the end of the string. He would dangle the apple into the orchestra pit and pretend to be fishing while Ernie stood looking somewhat bewilderedly at the sight that met his eyes. The joke then proceeded as follows:

Ernie: What are you doing?
Eric: Fishing.
Ernie: You don't catch fish with an apple, you catch fish with a worm.
Eric: That's all right, the worm's inside the apple.

Incidentally, Vince Powell, who sadly died in 2009, believed he was one of the first people, if not the first, to write for Eric and Ernie. He explained that he went backstage to meet the double act after one of their performances during their touring days. Asked what he wanted, Vince cheekily told them they both needed new material and offered to write for them. He went home and stayed up all night writing the kind of material he felt would suit them. He returned the next day and showed Eric the result of his nocturnal efforts. Eric is said to have turned to Ernie and said, 'Pay the man.' Vince would later go on to write early episodes of *Coronation Street* and material for performers including Cilla Black, Bruce Forsyth, and Mike and Bernie Winters. His sitcom credits, meanwhile, included *George and the Dragon*, *Nearest and Dearest* and *Bless This House.* Vince's comedy writing partner, until his untimely death in 1973, was Harry Driver.

A defining moment in the history of Eric and Ernie's double act took place when the tour of *Youth Takes a Bow* was visiting the Midlands in 1941. Put simply, the singer Adelaide Hall's husband, Bert Hicks, suggested that Eric changed his second name to the place where he was born. From then on, Eric Bartholomew became Eric Morecambe and Bartholomew and Wise became Morecambe and Wise. It seemed the best solution to an ongoing discussion as to a better name for the act. Eric's use of the seaside town's name as the second part of his professional name would inspire many a memorable line over the coming years. For instance, when Eric reminded former Prime Minister Harold Wilson that his name was Morecambe and not Ramsgate in a

Christmas special in 1978, Harold quipped, 'I knew you were getting on for the last resort.'

Youth Takes a Bow cast member Mary Naylor remembers just how close the two boys became on the tour. 'There was such a tremendous bond between Ernie and Eric that nobody would ever break, ever, ever, ever,' she said. 'I must say, in my humble opinion from growing up with them and seeing them as performers, I truly don't think that Eric would have made it without Ernie, and I don't think Ernie would have made it without Eric.'

The tour of *Youth Takes a Bow* came to an end in 1942 and Eric and Ernie went their separate ways. Despite this setback, the occasional opportunities Michie and Hylton had given them to perform as a double act were to prove invaluable.

2

A Couple of
Young Funsters

AFTER A QUIET SPELL on the performing front, during which Eric took a day job in a factory in Lancashire, and Ernie found himself delivering coal again in Yorkshire, Morecambe and Wise found themselves appearing in *Strike a New Note* at the Prince of Wales Theatre in London. This was thanks to the tenacity of Sadie who arranged them an audition with an agent, whose identity remains a mystery. He suggested they audition for George Black who was preparing for a new show. Black was born on 20 April 1890 in Small Heath, Birmingham. He became a hugely successful impresario. He had tenures of theatres including The London Palladium on Argyll Street and the Hippodrome Theatre on Cranbourn Street, Leicester Square. Ernie had the good fortune to meet George on occasions back in the days when he was staying at Jack Hylton's home in West Sussex. This seemed like a good omen.

Sadie, Eric and Ernie made their way to audition for *Strike a New Note* the following week at the Hippodrome Theatre.˙ However, there was a problem. George Black didn't want Eric and Ernie to perform as a double act. For Eric, to work in a theatre again, far away from the razor-blade factory he had been subjected to, would have been sufficient. This compromise wasn't good enough for Ernie, though, who risked losing them both the offered engagement by telling their potential new employer how he felt.

Luckily, George backed down. He agreed that Eric and Ernie could perform a routine together as a double act if one of the comedians in the show was unable to go on. This was not the last time that Ernie's drive and

---

˙ Ironically, despite their later fame and success at the box office, Eric and Ernie refused to play the venue years later when it became Bernard Delfont's stylish cabaret venue, The Talk of the Town. Officially, this was because the boys didn't like performing to the sound of people clinking cutlery and glasses, but it's rumoured that Delfont's financial offer to Morecambe and Wise was the real reason why they never performed there.

belief would benefit the comedy partners. No doubt Sadie, who had decided to accompany the act down to London in search of future engagements, must have felt proud of the way Ernie had handled the situation.

Strike a New Note opened on 18 March 1943 and played Mondays to Saturdays twice daily at 2.40pm and 5.30pm. The cast included the comedian and singer Derek Roy. Roy's career credits included appearing on the BBC radio show *Hip-Hip-Hoo-Roy*, and hosting the BBC radio talent programme *Variety Bandbox*, a series on which Morecambe and Wise were destined to appear.

The comedy entertainer Sid Field was also part of the company. Despite his obvious talents, Field toured the music halls of the provinces for years before finally finding success. His character 'Slasher Green', the Cockney spiv, caught the public's attention, and he was to star in *Strike it Again* and *Piccadilly Hayride*, as well as *Strike a New Note*. Field left the entertainment world stunned when he died on 3 February 1950 aged just forty-six. Never far from Sid's side on stage was his straight man, Jerry Desmonde, who would later find more success appearing with Norman Wisdom in a small number of Rank films including *I'll Follow a Star* and *The Early Bird*. Tragically, he took his own life on 11 February 1967 aged fifty-eight.

On 16 April 1943, Eric and Ernie could be heard performing on a radio version of *Strike a New Note* on the Forces Programme, a BBC radio station which operated from 7 January 1940 until 26 February 1944.

Even though *Strike a New Note* did not give Morecambe and Wise any performance experience as a double act, it did at least give them the opportunity to meet some of the biggest names in showbiz, as many of these stars came to see the show and their friends in the cast. Exciting it may have been, but Eric and Ernie were still convinced that working together as a double act was the way forward. Wherever possible, they appeared on stage in other shows to get further experience. The year 1943 also saw them engaged to perform in editions of the radio series *Youth Must Have its Fling* on the BBC Home Service. They were slowly making their way and learning to respect each other's equally important roles in the act.

Although working as entertainers was paramount to Morecambe and Wise, there was a war to be won. Ernie received his call-up papers in 1943, and went on to spend the following two years serving in the Merchant Navy helping to deliver coal from up north to Battersea Power Station in London. Eric, too, did not escape being called up, but being younger meant he was able to stay with *Strike a New Note* until the run ended. A spell as a straight man to comedian Gus Morris in ENSA (Entertainments National Service Association) occupied his time until his turn came to serve king and country.

A continued supply of coal was an obvious necessity to the war effort, and with millions of miners having left their posts to serve in the forces, replacements were desperately needed. With volunteers few and far between, the Minister of Labour and National Service in the wartime coalition government, Ernest Bevin, launched a scheme that would see one in ten males between the ages of eighteen and twenty-five called up to work in the mines. Between December 1943 and March 1948, around forty-eight thousand young men found themselves working as 'Bevin Boys'.

Eric's call-up in 1944 saw him working down the mines as a Bevin Boy in Accrington. It was not a popular scheme amongst most of those picked and denied the opportunity of, say, joining the Army, the Navy or the RAF. For Eric, the harsh working environment caused what would be the start of lifelong health problems, and resulted in him being invalided out in 1945. Arguably, the heart trouble he experienced may have contributed to the heart problems he would have later in his life. Another spell in a Morecambe razor-blade factory gave Eric a further chance to help his country in its hour of need.

Eventually Eric, thanks to Sadie's assistance, was offered an engagement as a feed to comedian Billy Revell in a touring show. Ernie, meanwhile, thanks to contacts he had made in the business, found and took on his own solo performing engagements around the country when they were available. But if Morecambe and Wise were now considering working apart again permanently, Sadie had other ideas. A coincidental meeting on Regent Street in London in 1946 saw Sadie persuade the two young men to live and work together again.

In 1947, thanks to Sadie's unofficial managerial efforts, Eric and Ernie were found work on *Lord John Sanger's Circus and Variety Tour*. During the tour, which used a large circus tent as a venue to seat an audience of seven hundred people, neither the poor selection of animals nor the variety acts seemed to impress the small number of punters who attended the performances. As if things weren't difficult enough for the double act, they found their favoured roles of comic and feed being reversed. Comedy-wise, the tour called upon Eric and Ernie to appear in a sketch called 'The Nursing Home'. Eric played the Doctor and Ernie played the Patient while a performer called Molly Seddon played the Nurse. To say the least, the comedy material in the show was thin and, not surprisingly, the resulting laughs few and far between. Although Morecambe and Wise's long-term agreement was to always share the money fifty-fifty, Ernie was paid two pounds more than his partner. Worse still, due to poor business their wages were cut down to seven and five pounds respectively. Edward Sanger, who employed all the performers, also expected them to help with fitting up and striking the tent at wherever this ill-thought-out production limped on to next.

The only redeeming aspect of the Sanger saga was that it resulted in Ernie meeting his future wife, Doreen Blythe. 'Eric and Ernie were doing their act and there were four girls dancing in the show, including me,' said Doreen. 'At first, I thought he was a wolf and didn't like him, but he would set out on his bike to hunt out food for the circus – he was great at organising and catering and I guess a sort of cupboard love grew between us. He used to say, "Do you think you could wash this shirt for me?" and some sweets would sail through the window. Then, when I knew him better, I found that he wasn't a wolf, it was just that he liked people. He really would have been a marvellous social worker. Anyway, he invited me to the cinema. I didn't enjoy it very much. It was an early Margaret Lockwood film, and every now and again someone would dash on and say, "There's trouble at the mine!" So, for the rest of the show, that became our pet phrase.'

The ill-fated Sanger tour ended at the annual Goose Fair in Nottingham in 1947. Eric and Ernie then travelled down to Chiswick in London to check into digs. Down but not out, the act realised they would simply have to put the disastrous tour down to experience and move onwards and upwards.

With Sadie, their unofficial manager, back home in Morecambe, Eric and Ernie realised they had to find new bookings and quickly if their act was to succeed and, more importantly, if they were to keep eating! It didn't take them long to realise that having an agent was the best way to obtain bookings. However, getting an agent was proving difficult, as they wanted to see Morecambe and Wise working before they would consider whether to take them on their books. Equally frustrating was the fact that many of the bigger variety theatres wouldn't book Eric and Ernie unless they had an agent. Fortunately, an ENSA tour of American army camps in Germany was one of the engagements that did come their way.

Ernie had continued to keep in touch with Doreen Blythe since their days touring with *Lord John Sanger's Circus and Variety Tour*. 'It was purely platonic though,' explained Doreen. 'He had another girlfriend he was always talking about, and I had other boyfriends. But all at once it wasn't platonic any more. He had just come back after entertaining the Americans in Germany, and when I told him I was going to Canada to do a dancing act he seemed very annoyed that I was going.'

In 1948, Morecambe and Wise were faced with a temporary name change while they were appearing in variety at the Palace, Walthamstow. The bill included an act that went by the name of Vic Wise and Nita Lane –

'The weak guy and his weakness'. Vic was not happy at the prospect of there being two Wises on the bill. To appease him, Ernie changed his surname to Wisdom. A poster for the twice-nightly show, which began on Monday 8 March, billed the duo as Morecambe and Wisdom – 'Just two guys'.

There were two radio show bookings of note for Morecambe and Wise in 1948, which saw them take part in individual broadcasts of *Beginners, Please!* and *Show Time* on the BBC Light Programme. More importantly, on 21 April, Eric and Ernie were given the chance to audition for BBC television at the Star Sound Studios on Baker Street in London. Given the content and huge success of their later television shows, the following notes made at their audition have more than a touch of irony about them:

> … Parts of this act might be suitable for television. Suggestive material and dancing together should be omitted.

Unfortunately, bookings for Morecambe and Wise to appear on BBC television were not destined to follow until the early part of the next decade.

Their luck did appear to be improving, however, when they found themselves engaged to work at the infamous Windmill Theatre situated in Soho's Great Windmill Street in London. Although the theatre had opened on 15 June 1931 with a straightforward play called *Inquest*, the venue later became famous for Laura Henderson's *Revudeville*, complete with static nude tableaus. That said, its contribution to the world of comedy and variety was considerable. Performers including Jimmy Edwards, Tony Hancock, Spike Milligan, Harry Secombe, Peter Sellers, Michael Bentine, George Martin, Bruce Forsyth, Arthur English, Tommy Cooper and Barry Cryer were all engaged at one time or another by the Windmill's owner, Vivian Van Damm, who had been left the theatre by Laura Henderson in her will.

Unfortunately, Morecambe and Wise's time at the Windmill Theatre was both mixed and short-lived. After just one week of performing in six shows a day, they were asked to leave by Vivian Van Damm (who, for some unknown reason, preferred to be known as VD!). Given that the audience at the Windmill was mostly made up of men more interested in studying the female dancers' figures rather than the comedic invention of the comedy performers on the bill, Morecambe and Wise could be forgiven for not playing to a wall of laughter.

Although their Windmill booking had not gone exactly to plan, it did at least bring Eric and Ernie into contact with an agent called Gordon Novel. Thanks to his timely intervention, Morecambe and Wise were booked to appear at the Clapham Grand in the dubiously titled *Fig Leaves and Apple Sauce*. At the time, the act had enough material to perform just one spot. This booking, however, required two. Their desire to fulfil this engagement resulted in the boys quickly devising a routine around 'The Woody Woodpecker Song'; and, although their first spot left the audience cold, the reception they received for the second offered them hope and saw offers for future bookings rolling in. Kilburn Empire was their workplace for the following week. They even came back to the Clapham Grand and were promoted to top of the bill.

The boys' variety engagements in 1949 included a week's appearance that April at Feldman's Theatre in Blackpool. This prompted a reviewer for the *Blackpool Gazette* to reward the duo with the quote:

> Morecambe and Wise, a couple of young funsters, have
> a promising style and a good comedy line.

By the end of the year, Eric and Ernie were appearing at the Royal Opera House in Leicester, playing Jimmy Green and Johnny Stout respectively in Prince Littler's production of the Christmas pantomime *Red Riding Hood*. The cast included Freddie Frinton, who would go on to appear with Thora Hird in the sitcom *Meet the Wife*, as Dame Trott (Red Riding Hood's grandma). Pantomime became an important part of Morecambe and Wise's early years. 'It was solid bread and butter,' explained Ernie. 'But it sometimes meant virtually living in crummy dressing-rooms. You'd find cracked mirrors, old wardrobes with no hangers, springs sticking out of the settee and filthy carpets – if any carpet at all.'

On 20 March 1950, Eric and Ernie began a week's booking at the Birmingham Hippodrome. The bill for the twice-nightly variety show, which had performances at 6.15pm and 8.30pm, included 'Monsewer' Eddie Gray, Jimmy James and Anne Shelton. Other variety dates that year included a week at the Liverpool Empire, which commenced on 17 April. The twice-nightly bill also included the then future Doctor Who, Jon Pertwee, and 'Hollywood dynamic film stars', Peggy Ryan and Ray McDonald. Morecambe and Wise also joined *Front Page Personalities* in 1950, thanks to Doreen Blythe, who was one of the cast members of this touring revue.

The duo parted company with Gordon Novel in the latter part of 1950, and Frank Pope become their new agent. It might have seemed a ruthless move after all of Novel's invaluable help, but Pope had the power to get bookings on the Moss Empires circuit – including the notorious Glasgow Empire, which was known as 'the English comedians' graveyard'. Eric and Ernie realised they needed to improve their billing, and thus their fees, if they were to continue working steadily as a double act. But although their decision to sign to Pope would turn out to be a beneficial one, the act did indeed struggle to generate laughter at the Glasgow Empire when their time came to perform there. In 1984, Ernie recalled the days they played the infamous theatre. 'We went on in silence and did the whole act in about four minutes flat and came off and the fireman said, "They're beginning to like you."'

Christmas 1950 saw Eric and Ernie appearing in the pantomime *Red Riding Hood* at the Golders Green Hippodrome. The production's cast also included Reg Varney (later to find fame in the LWT sitcom *On the Buses*), Leo Franklyn, Rosalind Melville and Doreen Lavender.

Morecambe and Wise returned to the Birmingham Hippodrome the following year for another week's variety which commenced on 9 April 1951. This time the bill included Michael Bentine. The year also saw Eric and Ernie finally make their television debut. Although their appearance on *Parade of Youth*, a long-forgotten talent programme, on 28 September 1951 didn't exactly set the world on fire, a later appearance on *Blackpool Stars* did.

On 22 October 1951, Eric and Ernie began a week's twice-nightly variety at the Shepherd's Bush Empire in London. Lee Lawrence, billed as 'Britain's Outstanding Singing Star', together with his pianist, Len Taylor, was top of the bill, while then twenty-six-year-old comic Peter Sellers ('Radio's Peter Sellers') was second. The cast also included Billy Thorburn ('Radio's Ace Pianist'), Chuck Brown and Rita ('American Novelty Act') and the Richard Sisters, together with Jose Moreno and Assistant. The following evening, 23 October 1951, highlights of the show (including Lawrence, Sellers, and Morecambe and Wise) went out live on the BBC Home Service in a weekly programme called *First House: Vaudeville* which featured broadcasts from famous music halls and theatres. The show was introduced from the Shepherd's Bush Empire by Brian Johnston, who became best known as a cricket commentator.

Christmas that year saw Eric and Ernie appearing in *Red Riding Hood* at the Empire Theatre, Dewsbury. During the run of the pantomime, Ernie bought Doreen an engagement ring for eighty pounds at F. Diss and Sons' jewellers in Market Place. He later proposed to Doreen on Valentine's Day 1952.

Morecambe and Wise appeared at the Birmingham Hippodrome for the week commencing Monday 7 April 1952. The twice-nightly variety show was called *Peek-a-Boo* and, amongst others, Michael Bentine and Phyllis Dixey were on the bill. The double act also accepted guest spots on the radio programmes *Workers' Playtime*, *Variety Bandbox* and *Variety Fanfare*.

In June 1952, Eric met his future wife, Joan Bartlett, at the Empire Theatre, Edinburgh. Joan, who spent five years of her early life in Burma due to her father being in the army, once described herself as 'an accident of showbiz'. Joan loved amateur dramatics and, like Eric and Ernie, was smitten by show business. Eventually the modelling engagements she had been receiving were replaced with offers to appear as a soubrette in touring variety shows. That day in 1952, Joan had only just arrived at the theatre and put her band parts down at the morning band call when Eric said to Ernie, 'That's the girl I'm going to marry.'

For Eric, at least, it was instant attraction; for Joan it was not. However, faint heart never won fair lady, and Eric decided persistence was the answer if he was going to win Joan's heart. 'Eric instantly took a shine to me, so that I thought: Now hold on a moment, what's going on here?' Joan said. 'I stepped back from him for a time. Having said that, you only played these theatres for a week and then you moved on to another theatre. You can get very bored in the daytime when the shows are in the evening. You've got the morning and part of the afternoon to kill. Invariably, people used to go to the cinema in the afternoon. Eric persisted and it started with us having coffee in the morning. He didn't give up as he was quite a determined person. I went to the cinema with both Eric and Ernie and it sort of carried on from there.'

Joan's knowledge of the double act was limited prior to meeting them. 'I didn't know anything about

Morecambe and Wise at the time,' she said. 'I'd vaguely heard their names and I guess I thought they were a couple of pianists or something.' Even in the early days, Joan was convinced that Eric and Ernie had tremendous potential. She would watch them from the wings while they were on stage. 'They were full of get-up-and-go and terribly keen, and they just loved show business,' said Joan. 'And, of course, you have this great enthusiasm when you're young. But do you know, I never doubted that Eric would get to the top. It never even crossed my mind that he wouldn't. I took it for granted. I just couldn't see anything else for them. Eric never just relied on words. He was a funny person and I think that's when you get the true comic. And, of course, Ernie brilliantly complemented him.'

Fate took a hand to ensure that Eric and Joan stayed in touch after the run at the Empire ended. Eric and Ernie were due to perform in Margate, Joan's home town. She recommended that Eric and half of the Billy Cotton Band Show stay with her parents and brother at the hotel they ran together. Meanwhile, as Joan was scheduled to work at a theatre in Morecambe, Eric arranged for her to stay with his parents.

Eric and Joan married on 11 December 1952, with Ernie taking on the role of best man. Eric later joked that marriage to Joan was just one of his many hobbies. 'But this one I didn't get rid of so easily,' he quipped. 'I had a week out from the theatre and nothing to do, so I thought I'd get married.' A plaque outside the Bull's Head public house in Margate, Kent, commemorates the fact that Eric and Joan held their wedding reception there.

Christmas 1952 saw the double act appearing as Captain and Mate in John Beaumont's 'Magnificent Yorkshire Comedy Pantomime' *Dick Whittington and His Cat* at Sheffield Lyceum Theatre. The cast also featured David Kerr and Ken Platt.

Despite being engaged to Doreen, the announcement of Eric and Joan's engagement and wedding took Ernie somewhat by surprise. 'I think he was shell-shocked that Eric got married so quickly as we did,' observed Joan. 'It wasn't sensible, to be honest. I think he visualised that there had always been two of them and now it would be Eric and wife and not Eric and Ernie. But I never ever wanted to interfere with their lives. I never ever tried to separate them in any way.'

Ernie's concern for looking after the pounds, shillings and pence remained uppermost in his mind even when it came to his wedding. He was adamant that he and Doreen weren't going to get married until he felt they were comfortable. But the best-laid plans don't always come to fruition. 'When he had nine hundred and ninety pounds in the bank, he drew it all out to buy a car,' Doreen recalled, 'and when we married, we had to stay in my mother's back bedroom.'

Ernie and Doreen married in Peterborough on 18 January 1953. This time, Eric was Ernie's best man. The couple were married by special licence because it was a Sunday. Doreen said, 'I spent the rest of that Sunday freezing to death in Sheffield, and the next afternoon I was sitting in a theatre box watching the boys in a pantomime.' Eventually, Ernie and Doreen found the time to go on a proper honeymoon to Paris.

When their finances recovered, the couple moved into their own home on Thorpe Avenue, off Thorpe Road, in Peterborough. Their neighbour was Ernie's friend and fellow performer, Edmund Hockridge. Ernie and Doreen decided they would never have children. 'Ernie always said that as soon as children are involved, the wife stays at home, and that way trouble lies,' explained Doreen. 'He knew about the temptations of being on the road. And I knew that I could never have tolerated infidelity.' Various dogs did, however, share their lives together, including a Scottie called Boots.

On 6 March 1953, Morecambe and Wise took part in a Grand Variety and Ice Gala at the Grand Theatre, Leeds. The 2.00pm performance, which featured the stars from the Leeds and Sheffield combined theatres, raised funds for the 'Lord Mayor's Flood Relief Fund'. Albert Modley, Ken Platt, Albert Rae and the Tiller Girls were just some of the other performers who appeared.

The London Palladium beckoned for Eric and Ernie the following month. The two-week booking, which commenced on Monday 6 April, saw them appearing alongside the Beverley Sisters, Zero Mostel (his first time in England) and Florence Desmond, who had appeared in two films with George Formby, one of Eric's comedy heroes.

Beginning on 1 June, Eric and Ernie returned to the Birmingham Hippodrome for another week of twice-nightly performances. The other acts on the bill included Ken Platt and Harry Worth. That summer saw the performers appear in George and Alfred Black's production of *Something to Sing About* at the Winter Gardens in Blackpool. The cast of this summer show also included Allan Jones, Ken Platt and Harry Worth. Bill Burgess of the *Blackpool Gazette* gave a glowing review for the comedians:

> Particular mention must be made of Morecambe and Wise. How do we define their act? It is an adroit blend of wry humour and the unexpected comeback, launched on immaculate timing and likeable personalities.

Eric's daughter, Gail Bartholomew, was born on Monday 14 September 1953, while *Something to Sing About* was still running. Eric recalled her birth in a 1973 interview: 'On Sunday 13 September 1953, my wife

Joan started to give birth to our first child. We were living at my parents' place in Morecambe, and I was appearing in Blackpool, less than thirty miles away. While we were on stage, I saw someone mouthing at me from the wings, "It's a girl!" I was given permission to leave the theatre before the finale.

'When the cast were all lined up after the curtain calls, Allan Jones stepped forward and said, "Ladies and gentlemen, I have an announcement to make. You'll notice that Eric Morecambe of Morecambe and Wise – that wonderful double act on the bill – was not with us for the finale. Well, folks, there's a good reason. He's rushing home this very minute to his wife, because he has just become the father of a six-month baby girl." I'm told those were his very words!'

Following Gail's birth, the couple decided to buy and stay in a caravan while Eric was touring with Ernie. It made life far from easy. He explained, 'We had to learn to adapt ourselves to a gypsy life, especially in a northern city during the winter, with nowhere to park the caravan, no sanitary arrangements, no running water and a pile of dirty nappies. Under such conditions caravanning was penitential. It played havoc with my nerves, not to mention my driving.'

Eric and Joan later decided that life on the road was no place for children. 'In our early days in pantomime, Joan and I soon had to decide on the sort of home life we would make for ourselves and our children,' Eric explained. 'Show business creates problems that just don't exist for people outside it. This was brought home to me one day when Joan came backstage with Gail and a couple of chorus girls started making a fuss of the child. They made her up with lipstick, rouge and a beauty spot. Gail was in her element, but I had a vision at that moment of the possibility of her growing up as a showbiz child, spoilt and precocious. After that I put a block on her being brought backstage. She would be a normal child, have a normal home life, and a normal schooling.'

The year 1953 also saw Eric and Ernie perform in editions of the radio programmes *Variety Fanfare*, *Workers' Playtime*, *Blackpool Night* and *Variety Playhouse*. Due to their success on the variety circuit and having made guest spots on several radio shows, Morecambe and Wise were given their own radio series called *YoYo (You're Only Young Once)*. A total of three series, thirty episodes in all, were made. The first was broadcast on 9 November 1953, while the last edition hit the airwaves on 17 December 1954. Many of the episodes of *YoYo* were produced by Johnny Ammonds, who would later become a major part of Eric and Ernie's television success, while he was also working with the likes of Jimmy Clitheroe. Ronnie Taylor also produced certain editions of the series.

Johnny Ammonds was aware of, and an admirer of, Morecambe and Wise's many variety theatre appearances. Despite the duo's opinions on their radio work, Johnny believed they took to radio like ducks to water. Material for *YoYo* (*You're Only Young Once*) was written as a joint effort between the show's writer Frank Roscoe and the double act. Johnny Ammonds and Ronnie Taylor also brought ideas to the table. Over the years Eric and Ernie had collated numerous jokes heard while on the variety circuit, and many of these were interwoven into the scripts.

The radio shows were recorded on Sundays in Manchester, allowing Eric and Ernie to continue touring theatres during the week. It was a tiring schedule and meant they were working seven days a week. Fleshing out Roscoe's scripts was essential but added to their stressful schedule, as it could only be done just hours before the shows were recorded, and they had to work fast to ensure they had time to rehearse before the audience arrived. Episodes were based around the fictitious 'Morecambe and Wise Detective Agency', a premise which gave an excuse for a guest to be brought into the story each week to request the services of the detectives; the various guests included Charlie Chester, Deryck Guyler and Harry Secombe.

Out of all the mediums Eric and Ernie were to work in, radio was surprisingly not Eric's favourite. 'I enjoy television very much, I enjoy theatre very much, I enjoy radio the least and yet that's the easiest because you can read and I'm not a very good reader, you see,' said Eric in 1978. One imagines Eric's frustration with the medium was down to the fact that it was harder to convey a facial expression, a look, a grimace on the radio. Yes, the studio audience could see them, but the audience at home couldn't. Eric's son, Gary, once said that he believed his father and Ernie compensated for this by speaking louder and faster.

Despite their successful radio appearances, Ernie was never convinced the medium was where they made their mark. 'We were never really radio comedians,' he said. 'We never really made any big impact on the radio, not in the sense of Hancock and Tommy Handley. We never really had a hit show.' Yet the double act would continue recording their own radio shows until 1978.

Christmas 1953 saw Morecambe and Wise return to the Sheffield Lyceum Theatre to play the Robbers, Marmaduke and Horace respectively, in *Babes in the Wood*. The cast for the pantomime, which began on Thursday 24 December, also included Mary Millar, David Kerr and Stan Stennett. Stan later recalled his memories of meeting the double act for the first time. 'It was the fifties, the early fifties, that I met my great friends Eric and Ernie – Morecambe and Wise. And we met in pantomime and we hit it off right away. We had something in common. Right from the start, from the very morning we met at the rehearsal, there was some chemistry about it that made it work for us.'

Eric and Ernie made an appearance on the television show *Stars in Blackpool* during 1953. It was this programme that led them to meeting the head of light entertainment at the BBC, Ronnie Waldman. No one realised it at the time, but this meeting would turn out to be one of the most important in television history.

3
Running Wild

RADIO CONTINUED TO BE a major employer for Morecambe and Wise in 1954. In addition to their own series *YoYo* (*You're Only Young Once*) continuing, they also made further editions of *Variety Fanfare, Workers' Playtime* and *Blackpool Night*. They were asked to perform on *Henry Hall's Guest Night* and *Having a Wonderful Time*. The year also saw Eric and Ernie offered the chance to make their own television series called *Running Wild*.

Ronnie Waldman at the BBC believed the double act were made for television, and who were Eric and Ernie to argue? Television was a medium they knew they had to get established in. *TV Mirror* magazine featured Eric and Ernie as they prepared for the first edition of *Running Wild*. While they might have been nervous, the extracts from this interview perceive them as being optimistic about the outcome of the experience:

The Lads Who've Got Nothing to Lose

Morecambe and Wise, the young comedians from the North, have gained a big reputation on radio. Tonight, they begin a new comedy series on television.

Ever since it was announced that a new fortnightly comedy series starring Morecambe and Wise was starting, the two bright lads from the North have been receiving good advice from their colleagues and friends.

'You keep off television – it'll do you no good,' was the general burden of their advice.

But Eric Bartholomew, who comes from Morecambe (hence the name), and Ernie Wiseman, who claims Leeds as his native town, think differently. After no fewer than forty-five appearances in *Variety Fanfare*, and their own weekly variety series, *You're Only Young Once*, they have no doubts about the power of sound radio to help an artist on his way.

And whatever the dismal Johnnies may say about the dangers of a television series that gets panned by the critics – well, Morecambe and Wise just aren't worrying.

'The way we look at it is this,' said Morecambe (he is the tall one with glasses). 'Television has come to stay, and we've been given our big opportunity. We'd be daft if we didn't take it with both hands. You see, we've got everything to gain and nothing to lose.'

'It isn't as though we were at the end of our careers,' added Wise (the small one with the fair hair). 'You're only young once, that's quite true. But we're young now, both of us. I'm twenty-eight and Eric is twenty-seven. And I'd say we've got a few years to go yet. If the public don't like us on Wednesday, that's just too bad. But it won't mean we're finished. Why, we've hardly started yet!'

'And there's another radio series starting in May to keep the wolf from the door,' said Morecambe.

I tried to find out something about the new television show. The two boys looked at each other, scratched their hair and seemed a little embarrassed. 'Well, it's a comedy show – we know that much. And it's a revue – there's no harm in telling you that. But as for what it's going to be – look, why don't you watch it and find out.'

'That's what we're going to do,' said Morecambe, changing the subject.

When I could get them talking seriously, I got some pretty definite opinions out of Morecambe about this new television series. 'It's like this,' he said, 'No one, with the possible exception of Arthur Askey, has yet managed to bring off a television series with any real success.'

'Now don't imagine that we're comparing ourselves with Askey – we don't wear the same size in combs. But we're prepared to look on television as a completely different medium. We're ready to change our approach and our styles as much as is wanted.'

It is my opinion that they will be a big success.

But while they were allowed considerable input into the radio scripts for *YoYo (You're Only Young Once),*

Morecambe and Wise were deprived of the same opportunity for *Running Wild*. That would be the biggest mistake with the making of this new, six-part series, which Bryan Sears was given the job of producing. Unfortunately, Sears was one of the producers at the BBC who felt Eric and Ernie's act and ideas would not translate to southern audiences on television, and he commissioned a small team of writers to work on the material for the series.

It's believed that Denis Goodwin and Bob Monkhouse were asked to supply material for the shows. That they never did remains a mystery. The writing partnership provided a prolific amount of funny material for their clients, as well as themselves when they worked together. Maybe their schedule was just too busy – we'll never know. But it does make one wonder if the series might have been more successful if they had.

The guests booked for *Running Wild* included Alma Cogan, vocal group The Four-in-a-Chord, Ray Buckingham, Marjorie Holmes, Hermione Harvey, Amanda Barrie, Bernard Bresslaw and Jill Day. There's no doubt that in this respect Eric and Ernie had brilliant support. However, when the first edition of *Running Wild* was broadcast on 21 April 1954, it was not declared a success by the critics of the day.

Eric would later offer his opinion on the problem performers have of establishing themselves. 'I feel very sorry for the comedians starting today, because they get thrown into the deep end before they've really had any experience. They have got nowhere to go and practise. They've got nowhere to go and be bad and nowhere to learn their trade.' It's true; back then comedians could play all the theatres and perform to all sorts of different types of audiences. Now, the nearest they have is a circuit of comedy clubs.

Eric and Ernie believed *Running Wild* was a good opportunity for them. But they didn't realise how much publicity it was going to get them! That it did is probably down to the fact that there was only one television channel at the time. Eric took all the cuttings out of the papers that contained negative reviews and kept them. This reminded him in later years, once Morecambe and Wise had achieved success in the medium, not to be complacent.

Arguably, the most famous of all the reviews for *Running Wild* went as follows: 'Definition of the week. TV set: The box they buried Morecambe and Wise in.'

An *Evening Standard* critic also offered their take on their first programme:

> After watching their *Running Wild* show last night, I was relieved – and disappointed. Relieved because in their way they are amusing. Disappointed because they are not more so. Theirs is the humour of the music hall sketch – a sketch we have seen a thousand times before.

What hurt Eric and Ernie was that they were doing what they were told by 'the experts', who knew what they wanted, and they did what they were given. Ironically, the director was Ernest Maxin. Maxin would later produce, direct and choreograph some of the double act's television programmes for the BBC.

Eric recalled that his mother, Sadie, wasn't pleased with the feedback *Running Wild* was getting. 'My mother telephoned from Morecambe. She'd seen some of the notices. "What the devil are you two playing at? I daren't show my face outside the house. We'll have to move; we'll have to change our name."'

Eric and Ernie and their agent, Frank Pope, attempted to get Ronnie Waldman to cancel the rest of the fortnightly series after just three editions. Each edition of *Running Wild* was broadcast from the BBC Television Theatre in Shepherd's Bush, London, where, of course, they had previously appeared in variety and taken part in the radio show *First House: Vaudeville*. Understandably, Eric and Ernie were concerned the failure of the series would affect the rest of their careers, and that their theatre and radio bookings would dry up. Waldman refused to cancel the rest of the series. He told them they were 'first-rate television comedy material' – in short, he still believed in them. Ironically, despite Waldman's views, no tapes of the six episodes were kept by the BBC.

Eric's wife, Joan, didn't agree with the critics' reception to the series. 'I don't think for a moment that it deserved the panning it got. But I think the press were waiting for someone to pounce on, because at the same time Bob Monkhouse was a tremendous hit. There was Bob riding high, with the press saying how marvellous he was, and there was Eric and Ernie, who were being slated.'

Many people have claimed that Eric lost all his confidence after *Running Wild* – but his wife later confirmed that he didn't. In fact, Eric and Ernie had to perform in a show at the Ardwick Hippodrome in Manchester in front of a live audience not long afterwards. Eric was a bit nervous of coming straight out of this flop for television and was concerned the audience wouldn't give them a warm welcome. On the contrary, they received a standing ovation. It was as if the audience wanted to show that they had sympathy for their recent experiences. This helped to boost the act's morale.

After the dust settled, Eric was not keen for him and Ernie to rush into doing any more television. They decided to take things slowly. They went back to doing what they knew best at that time – theatre and radio. Eric also suggested that they improve their act and work harder on getting their personalities across to the audience. Once they had become successful, Eric began seriously describing their act, but couldn't help but end on a line. 'It's two personalities complementing each other,' he said. 'I always call it high-class rubbish, that's what we do!'

Morecambe and Wise may have suffered a setback, but it was not all doom and gloom. One reviewer, Eric Littler, made some interesting comments in the *Blackpool Gazette* about a show he saw the duo appear in at the Palace Theatre, Blackpool, after their television series had ended:

> I am left wondering if they can possibly be the same two artistes who were in that television studio. They are, of course, but whatever the BBC did to them they have left it behind, and instead we have two performers whose slick humour had last night's first house audience rocking in their seats. It is the sort of material the whole family can enjoy… These two comedians are on the way up – provided they fight shy of television.

During July 1954, Morecambe and Wise supported the Beverley Sisters for a week at the Theatre Royal, Portsmouth. Also appearing in the show's company was Tommy Fields, who was the younger brother of Gracie Fields. Christmas that year saw the act appear in S. H. Newsome's 'Magnificent Pantomime' *Babes in the Wood* at the Hippodrome, Derby. They were given second billing while friend Stan Stennett was top of the bill. Also included in the cast were Gladys Joyce, Mary

Millar, Alan Curtis, Shirley Cook, Rex Holdsworth, Sandra and Mary, the Westway Corps de Ballet and the Welcome Singers.

The year 1955 brought more variety bookings for Eric and Ernie. For instance, the week commencing 21 March saw them appearing at the Bristol Hippodrome; Norman Vaughan, David Berglas and Harry Worth also appeared. The following week the double act moved to the Chiswick Empire to appear with Des O'Connor, Harry Worth and Joan Regan.

The same year saw the Royal Command Performance staged outside of London for the first time. Held in the presence of Queen Elizabeth II and the Duke of Edinburgh, the show took place at the Opera House in Blackpool on 13 April 1955. More importantly for Morecambe and Wise, it was the first time they had been invited to appear on the prestigious show. The cast that year included Reginald Dixon, Lupino Lane, George Truzzi, Peter Glaze, Kenneth Sandford, Pamela Bromley, Vera Day, the John Tiller Girls, the Victoria Palace Girls and Boys, Kathryn Moore, the Flying De Pauls, the Barbour Brothers and Jean, the Amandis, the Crazy Gang, Morecambe and Wise, Bill Waddington, Josephine Anne, the Showgirls, Arthur Askey, Geraldo and his Orchestra, Jewel and Warriss, Littlewoods Girls' Choir, Joan Regan, Alma Cogan, Five Smith Brothers, George Formby, 1st Battalion the Liverpool Scottish

(TA) (Queen's Own Cameron Highlanders), Beryl Grey with John Field, Jack Tripp, children from the Blackpool Tower Ballet, Charlie Cairoli with Paul, Wilfred and Mabel (Pickles), Albert Modley, Flanagan and Allen, Eddie Fisher with the BBC Northern Orchestra, and Al Read. For someone who had grown up inspired by George Formby and Arthur Askey, Eric must have been in his element to have been given the chance to appear on this same bill as both his comedy heroes. For Ernie, it was a chance to be reunited with Askey who he first performed with in the stage version of *Band Waggon* back in 1939.

The title of Eric and Ernie's 1955 summer season at the Central Pier, Blackpool, was *Let's Have Fun*. The comedy revue boasted Jimmy James, Jimmy Clitheroe and Roy Castle. The cast also featured an up-and-coming comedian called Ken Dodd, who was given a 'plum spot' in the second half of the twice-nightly show. Ken later reminisced about the run. 'I used to watch Morecambe and Wise from the wings each night for the first few months of the long run and watched the duo perform their quick-fire humour,' he said. 'Eric was like a playful imp. He had the perfect foil in Ernie. The foil or the "feed" is the man who builds the structure of the act – and Morecambe and Wise were an excellent double act. Comedians build their own base when they're on stage. Double acts are different as they build a situation.

A solo comedian can't do that as they feed off the audience. The audience is their straight man. I liked what they did, and they liked my act.'

Morecambe and Wise could also be heard on the airwaves again in 1955. They appeared on editions of *Spotlight, Workers' Playtime, The Show Goes On* and *Blackpool Night*. More importantly, this was the first year Eric and Ernie recorded programmes under the title *The Morecambe and Wise Show*. According to records, the first edition was broadcast on 19 October and the other two on 26 October and 2 November.

Eric and Joan's son, Gary Bartholomew, was born on 21 April 1956. This persuaded Gary's proud parents that changes needed to be made to their living arrangements. 'I had to take roots while Eric carried on working all over the country,' Joan once explained. 'There were long periods of being by myself with two babies and very little help, which is lonely when you are young. But as the children have got older it has become easier and easier.' Their new home was in a ground-floor flat in Finchley, north London; the house later become a nursing home.

Although there were no further editions of *The Morecambe and Wise Show* broadcast on the radio in 1956, Eric and Ernie did guest on the radio shows *Call Boy, Workers' Playtime, Variety Fanfare, Blackpool Night, Let's Make a Date, Mid-Day Music Hall* and *Variety Playhouse*. Eric and Ernie also joined the fun in a radio programme called *Morecambe Illuminations*, which, as you might have guessed, celebrated the turning on of the resort's annual summer illuminations.

Television bosses came knocking on Morecambe and Wise's door again in 1956. This time it was the turn of ITV, and the act were asked to perform on ATV's *The Winifred Atwell Show*. Eric and Ernie's first appearance on the series was broadcast on 21 April 1956 – exactly two years to the day after the first edition of *Running Wild*. All this and on the same day as Eric's wife gave birth to their second child! Eric and Ernie's spots were written by the future *Till Death Us Do Part* writer, Johnny Speight, who knew how to put their person-alities across.

Their first sketch in the series arguably secured Morecambe and Wise's future in television. Had the edition been recorded, then the 'happening' wouldn't have been witnessed by the viewers. It was another piece of luck that went in the duo's favour. And if luck needs a push, then in this case it was Ernie who pushed it. It was a sketch that involved a taxi, with Ernie playing the driver of said taxi. Following the tag, Ernie was meant to appear to drive the car out of vision with the aid of some stagehands who had attached a rope to the car. The problem was that Ernie, out of force of habit, put the car into gear – and try as much they could, the stagehands could not move the car. And that's when the glorious and hilarious ad-libbing between Eric and Ernie began. Such was the success of this unplanned piece of fun that intentional 'mistakes' were built into their subsequent appearances on the series.

Regional television was first broadcast in the Midlands of England on 17 February 1956 with the launch of ATV's weekday ITV service. Three months later, the first news programme, a daily five-minute bulletin called *ATV Midlands News*, was broadcast on 7 May 1956. ATV covered many of Eric and Ernie's visits to the Midlands. The earliest surviving footage, which was first shown on 1 February 1957, shows Eric and Ernie opening Leslie's electrical shop in Kidderminster. Before cutting the ribbon to declare the shop open, Eric chose the opportunity to cut Ernie's tie in half, much to the delight of the assembled crowd.

The double act supported singer Yana on her first variety tour in Britain in 1956. They played a week at each of the theatres on the tour, including the Empire Theatre, Nottingham, Birmingham Hippodrome, Palace Theatre, Manchester, and Coventry Theatre (previously known as the Coventry Hippodrome). Then, from 17 September, Eric and Ernie took part in a week's variety at the Savoy Theatre in Lincoln, supporting Joan Regan. The other cast members included the Lane Twins, Tattersall with Jerry and Co, Walthon and Dorraine, Sally Barnes and George Meaton.

Firework night 1956 saw the comedy duo begin two weeks' variety at the Prince of Wales Theatre in London's West End. Topping the bill was Hylda Baker, who would go on to play Nellie Pledge in the Granada Television sitcom *Nearest and Dearest*. This show was part of a season of variety being presented at the theatre by Val Parnell and Bernard Delfont. The bill also included Peggy Ryan and Ray McDonald, Charlie Cairoli and Derek Roy. An advert at the bottom of the poster boasted that Gracie Fields was set to follow the show and appear at the theatre for two weeks from 19 November 1956. Eric and Ernie ended the year by reuniting with old friend Stan Stennett to appear in *Dick Whittington* at Dudley Hippodrome.

In 1957, the BBC called upon the comedy duo to return to the small screen and booked them to appear on editions of a high-speed revue called *Double Six*. John Gower, Ted Lune, Eileen Dyson and the Jack Billings Dancers also appeared in the series. The same year also saw Morecambe and Wise bring their special brand of humour back to radio audiences for yet more editions of *Mid-day Music Hall*, *Workers' Playtime*, *Henry Hall's Guest Night*, *Call Boy* and *Blackpool Night*. They also made first guest outings on *By the Fireside* and *Star Train*.

Eric and Ernie returned to the Central Pier, Blackpool, for the summer season in 1957 in a new version of *Let's Have Fun*. Commencing on Saturday 1 June, the show, which ran Mondays to Saturdays at 6.10pm and 8.40pm, also featured Joan Turner, Maureen Rose, Three Duces, Eddie Grant, the Three Belles, the Orchid Room Lovelies, Kenny Baker and Dennis Spicer. On 3 June, BBC television broadcast an excerpt from the show in a programme called *Blackpool Show Parade Presents: Let's Have Fun*. This edition was produced by Barney Colehan, who also produced and directed the long-running series *The Good Old Days* for the BBC.

Pantomime in 1957 saw Morecambe and Wise appearing alongside Harry Secombe in *Puss in Boots* at the Coventry Theatre. The role of Puss in Boots was played by Gillian Lynne, who would go on to choreograph West End musicals including *CATS* and *The Phantom of the Opera*. This was her first principal role on stage.

On 6 February 1958, *ATV Midlands News* first showed footage filmed at a pantomime ball and press reception for the Birmingham-born actress Anne Heywood. Surviving footage includes Eric Morecambe, who holds his glasses to his knee (arguably one of the earliest surviving pieces of footage of Eric performing this gag), and Ernie Wise looking relaxed and joking with a group of fellow guests.

Summer season in 1958 saw Eric and Ernie support Alma Cogan at the Winter Gardens in Eric's home town of Morecambe. Entitled *Light Up the Town*, the show began its run on 8 July 1958 with a bill that also included Ken Platt and Semprini.

Following their summer season, Morecambe and Wise toured Australia for six months. According to research, their live performances included appearing in a stage show called *Rocking the Town* at the Tivoli Theatre, Melbourne, Victoria, on 7 October and Tivoli Theatre, Sydney, New South Wales, on 15 December 1958. The show featured members of the cast of *The Winifred Atwell Show* back in England.

By the time Eric and Ernie returned home, show business was changing. Although long summer seasons were still possible, weekly variety was becoming less lucrative to producers and performers as audiences dwindled and many theatres closed. 'We weren't the only people who had lost ground,' Ernie later explained to a journalist. 'What had happened during our absence was the beginning of a drastic change on the entertainment scene in Britain. Variety theatres had begun shutting their doors. Television was now the big entertainment medium of the future, so Eric and I sat down and thrashed out the situation.'

The double act continued to keep a high profile on the radio during 1958. The radio shows benefiting from their presence included further editions of *Call Boy*, *Workers' Playtime*, *Mid-day Music Hall*, *Blackpool Night* and, for the first time, *Laughter Incorporated*.

In 1959, Morecambe and Wise appeared in another summer season at the Central Pier in Blackpool. The *Blackpool Gazette* once more gave the boys a pleasing review:

> Eric, with his innocent vacuity and willingness to please, is the perfect foil for the bland, tolerant, worldly Ernie Wise, and the perfect vehicle for the misunderstandings and innuendos that get the laughs. It is difficult to see how it could be done better.

The act's other live dates in 1959 included appearing with Joan Regan and Billy Dainty in a week's variety, beginning 16 November, at the Finsbury Park Empire in London.

Leonard Sachs introduced Morecambe and Wise to the stage for a Christmas edition of *The Good Old Days*, first broadcast on Boxing Day 1959. Also appearing on the bill were Patricia Bredin, Cardew Robinson, Smoothey and Layton, Noberti, Betty Jumel and the Manton Bros. Eric and Ernie performed to an audience who, as was customary on this show, were dressed in period attire. This edition of the programme was one of two hundred and forty-five first broadcast by the BBC between 1953 and 1983. Christmas 1959 also saw the duo appearing as the Giant's Henchmen alongside Hylda Baker and Jimmy Clitheroe in *Jack and the Beanstalk* at the Empire Theatre, Liverpool.

The boys made yet another week-long appearance at the Birmingham Hippodrome in 1960. This time, they appeared twice-nightly in *The Michael Holliday Show,* which opened on 16 May. Away from the stage, the act's radio credits for the year included further guest spots on *Workers' Playtime* and *Mid-day Music Hall* as well as joining the line-up on *London Lights, Holiday Music Hall* and *Seaside Nights.*

Billy Marsh replaced Frank Pope as Morecambe and Wise's agent in 1960. Highly regarded in the business, Billy was working for Bernard Delfont's company, London Management, when he signed the duo. In 1987, he formed his own agency called Billy Marsh Associates. Sadly, he passed away on 19 November 1995. 'Billy said to them [Eric and Ernie], "Guys, if you're not on television, you don't exist in this business. You have to get on television," recalled Michael Grade. 'Billy talked my Uncle Lew [Lew Grade], who was ATV in those days, into giving them a few spots here and there."' This led to Eric and Ernie appearing on editions of programmes including *Sunday Night at the London Palladium, Saturday Night at the Prince of Wales* and *Saturday Spectacular* during the same year. All their hard work was finally paying off. But there was one thing missing: a television series of their own.

Christmas 1960 saw Eric and Ernie appearing in *Sinbad the Sailor* at the Alexandra Theatre in

Birmingham. The cast also included George Lacey, Anton and Janetta, Derek Royle (who would later play Mr Leeman, a hotel guest who dies, in an episode of *Fawlty Towers* called 'The Kipper and the Corpse'), the Four Playboys, Three Ghezzis and Lynette Rae.

Derek Royle's actress daughter, Carol Royle, has fond memories of this time. 'I remember Eric coming back to our flat in Sutton Coldfield,' she said. 'I was very young. He sat on our long red sofa and I stood behind him and brushed his hair – I used to brush everybody's hair!'

On 11 January 1961, Eric and Ernie took part in another film report for ATV in the Midlands. Silent footage has survived of the double act running onto the pitch of St Andrew's football ground in Birmingham before warming up and quickly running back inside. It's believed the item was shot as a way of making light of a proposed football players' strike that was in the news at the time.

Morecambe and Wise still managed to fit in a selection of radio broadcasts in 1961. They hit the airwaves in editions of *Workers' Playtime*, *From the Top*, *Seaside Nights*, *Flying High* and *In Town Today*. These engagements were cleverly shoehorned into their busy diary of live work. For instance, they opened in *Spring Show* at the Palace Theatre, Manchester, on 18 April 1961. The show, which also starred Alma Cogan, the Charlivels, the Dallas Boys, Rosemary Squires, Bill Dainty and Freddie Frinton, ran for six weeks.

Not long after the run finished, Eric and Ernie began preparing for that year's summer season at the Princess Theatre in Torquay. The cast of *Show Time* also included Tommy Cooper, Joan Regan and Edmund Hockridge. The first performance of the show co-incided with the opening of the theatre on Wednesday 7 June 1961.

It was during the same summer season that the double act first met Ann Hamilton, a soubrette and former Windmill girl who would go on to become the unofficial third member of Morecambe and Wise. Ann was appearing in a show at the nearby Pavilion Theatre with Jewel and Warriss. When both casts got together for parties, photos were taken that included Ann with Eric and Ernie. At the time, Ann didn't get a proper chance to talk to either of the two men or get to know them well. However, this would soon change. Hamilton would go on to work with the boys over a hundred times, prompting Eric Morecambe to refer to her as 'our Margaret Dumont'. This was a reference to the American stage and film actress who was the comic foil to the Marx Brothers in seven of their films. 'If you didn't fit in, you weren't asked back,' said Ann. Given her number of credits with Eric and Ernie, it's more than fair to say that Ann fitted in!

While they were appearing in summer season, Eric and Ernie were finally offered their own television series again. Yes, they had reservations about returning to the small screen with their own show, but ultimately both men knew that the medium of television was here to stay; and that, if they didn't embrace it, they would be left behind.

4

Breathless and Intoxicated

L EW GRADE OFFERED Eric and Ernie their own ATV series on the ITV network at four hundred pounds a week. According to BBC records, the corporation had also been keen for the double act to return to the bosom of Auntie. This would have been to work on a new six-part comedy series called *Four Aces and a King*. Frank Muir and Denis Norden, who were acting as consultants on the proposed series, sent the scripts to Morecambe and Wise. They seemed keen to do it – subject to the right deal, of course.

The reason the series didn't come to fruition is somewhat confusing. The then head of light entertainment at BBC television, Eric Maschwitz, and his deputy, Tom Sloan, were both involved in instigating the project. Neither man had any success in contacting Billy Marsh for a considerable time. By the time Marsh finally contacted both men, he claimed to know nothing of the BBC's intentions and informed them that Eric and Ernie would not be available – they had signed to ATV.

Eric and Ernie's first ATV series, entitled *Bernard Delfont Presents Morecambe and Wise*, featured nine thirty-minute editions and was broadcast live from the Wood Green Empire, then used as a television theatre, weekly starting on 12 October 1961. Sadly, none of these programmes have survived.

Colin Clews was brought in to produce and direct the series, and Sid Green and Dick Hills were hired as the writers – all at the request of Eric and Ernie. Their request was originally turned down but, after the double act threatened to back out of the series, a deal was done and Green and Hills were duly engaged as part of the production team. Eric and Ernie's guests for the first run of shows included the Confederates, Acker Bilk, the McGuire Sisters, the Peters Sisters, Cleo Laine, Gary Miller, Mickie Ashmon's Ragtime Jazz Band, Valerie Masters and the Kaye Sisters.

Sid Green and Dick Hills had written for the best, which is why Morecambe and Wise wanted them on board. Ironically, it was the material they wrote and submitted during the early part of the first series that caused some initial teething troubles. In short, Eric and Ernie were simply not happy with how many actors, actresses and extras Sid and Duck (as they nicknamed Dick) insisted on including in each of the sketches. The complaints fell on deaf ears and there was some initial tension in the rehearsal room.

Disappointingly, the reaction to the new series wasn't favourable; but then fate stepped in to stop *Running Wild* history repeating itself. Strike action by the acting union Equity meant that Morecambe and Wise were faced with the possibility of the rest of the series being postponed while the union's demands were discussed. But as with Bruce Forsyth and Norman Wisdom on their famous edition of *Sunday Night at the London Palladium* on 3 December 1961, Eric and Ernie got around the problem by virtue of not being members of Equity. Like Bruce and Norman, they belonged instead to the Variety Artistes' Federation (VAF). This meant that the series could continue – sans the epic number of performers that Sid and Dick were desperate to cram into the main sketches. At last the viewers could see more of Morecambe and Wise. Hills and Green even ended up performing in many of the sketches themselves, a state of affairs that continued even after the strike ended. One could summarise the events of series one by saying that, in life, a loss or misfortune usually benefits someone. In this case it benefited Morecambe and Wise – and the viewers.

At the start of each week, Sid and Dick would discuss ideas for sketches and routines with Eric and Ernie. From there, each show would be created. Part seriously, part humorously, Eric summed up the writing process for the ATV shows in 1966. 'We only need an idea, you see, and the four of us build from that,' he said. 'If we get a funny idea, like a BBC interview, we could work from that.'

They may have found a way of making things work during the writing process, but tensions would continue to erupt from time to time between Morecambe and Wise and Hills and Green. What probably helped make the situation more bearable was that the double act could still find humour in the situation. This can be proved with an extract from a newspaper interview in 1964 in which they shared their views on the making of their television shows. 'We've been called ad-lib comics,' said Wise. 'It isn't really that. It's just that we rehearse Tuesday, Wednesday, Thursday and Friday. And when we put the show together on Saturday, we still don't know it that well.' Eric added, 'Yes, those pauses... we're really thinking of what we are supposed to say next. The programme is often quite different from rehearsals – we've forgotten the script.'

The late actress and casting director Valerie Van Ost worked with Eric and Ernie at ATV. 'Although the shows were recorded before a live audience, there were always several runs before the audience were admitted,' she explained. 'Every time a sketch was rehearsed, the boys managed to add that little extra something that would have the crews falling about laughing. I had never seen such a spontaneous reaction to any comic I had ever worked with before. It was quite exceptional and made rehearsals great fun. I imagine that it was also a very useful gag-tester for Eric and Ernie.'

Eric, Joan and their two children, Gail and Gary, moved to their first of two homes in Harpenden in Hertfordshire during 1961. The same year saw Morecambe and Wise appear at the Prince of Wales Theatre in their second Royal Command Performance. The show, presented by Bernard Delfont, was staged in the presence of Queen Elizabeth the Queen Mother. Besides Eric and Ernie, the cast included Acker Bilk, Kenny Ball and the Temperance Seven, Shirley Bassey, Jack Benny, George Burns, Lionel Blair, Max Bygraves, Maurice Chevalier, the Crazy Gang, Sammy Davis Jr, Arthur Haynes, the McGuire Sisters, Nina and Frederik, Andy Stewart and Frankie Vaughan. The occasion marked Lionel Blair's first appearance in the annual show. 'When I did my first Royal Command Performance, performing with Sammy Davies Jr, Eric sent me a telegram,' Lionel remembered. 'It jokingly said, "I hear you're the only one getting paid!"'

The friendship Eric and Ernie shared with Lionel Blair was not new, however. 'When Joyce (my late sister) and I were appearing in *Kiss Me Kate* in Nottingham, Eric and Ernie were touring in variety and were also appearing in the city,' Lionel said. 'The theatres faced each other and so we used to have coffee together. Eric was lovely to us, but Joyce and I were always rowing at the time, and he used to tell us off.'

The year 1961 was rounded off for Eric and Ernie with them taking second billing to the singer David Whitfield in pantomime at the Grand Theatre, Leeds. Performances of *The Sleeping Beauty*, produced by Louis Barber, commenced on 26 December 1961 and ran until March 1962. The cast also included Patricia Lambert, Dorothy Dampier, Charlie Harris, Tony Heaton and Betty Emery.

The title of Eric and Ernie's second series for ATV was changed to *The Morecambe and Wise Show* (*Two of a Kind*) when it returned on 30 June 1962. Guests in the new run of thirteen thirty-minute editions included Terry Lightfoot's Jazzmen, the Beverley Sisters, Chris Barber's jazz band, Eric Delaney and his Band and Teddy Johnson and Pearl Carr.

June 1962 saw Morecambe and Wise open in the summer revue *Every Night at the London Palladium*, presented by Leslie A. Macdonnell and Bernard Delfont. Top of the bill was Bruce Forsyth. 'I knew Morecambe and Wise from when we were all struggling comics and we were often on the same bill together,' he recalled. 'When we were all performing in *Every Night at the London Palladium* together, I was top of the bill when it started. One of their television series was shown during the run. I could tell by the applause whenever they came on that they were becoming more popular because they were getting the same type of ovations I also used to get. At last they were finally receiving the success they deserved.'

The cast also included Eve Boswell, Teddy Johnson and Pearl Carr, and Janet Mahoney. Janet remembers that Eric and Ernie seemed to swap roles offstage. 'They were terrific,' she enthused. 'Ernie was funny offstage, but Eric was more serious, if I remember correctly. Of course, on stage Ernie was the straight man.'

It was during the run of *Every Night at the London Palladium* that Ed Sullivan, on one of his European talent-scouting missions, attended a performance. Liking Morecambe and Wise's act, he offered to fly them to New York so they could make an initial three appearances on his high-rating series *The Ed Sullivan Show* in 1963. They accepted the offer – and a reported five thousand pounds per show. It's become legendary that Sullivan initially made the mistake of introducing Morecambe and Wise as Moore, Cambe and Wise. When only Eric and Ernie bounded onto the stage, the audience would have been forgiven for wondering where the third performer was!

Their escapades across the Atlantic became the subject of a documentary series, *Morecambe and Wise in America*, on the UK TV channel GOLD. Footage of the act's first appearance on *The Ed Sullivan Show* reveals that the American studio audience were slow to catch on at first. It was a three-foot sword swallower gag that finally broke the ice and inspired some laughter in the Broadway theatre used for Sullivan's shows.

Explaining how the boys approached their bookings on the show, Eric's wife Joan said, 'They would do the show and then come back a couple of days later. They were always successful enough to be asked back by Ed Sullivan, who was an enormous name in America. But they only ever had these short spots. They didn't really have enough time for people to get to know their style.'

Although the double act would continue to make further appearances across the Atlantic up until 1968, including guesting on a ninety-minute spectacular to celebrate the eightieth birthday of Irving Berlin, they did not help Eric and Ernie to crack the American market. Joan remembers that her husband was never particularly interested in becoming successful in America. 'If it had just happened like that, fine. But Ernie felt very differently,' she recalled. 'He always had this little bit of an ambition to go to America, thinking back to the old days of Hollywood. He was living a little bit in the past, I always thought, because Hollywood was no longer like that. But I think he would have dropped everything and gone. Eric used to say, "It's taken us a lifetime to become stars in this country, so if we go and leave it and start working away for too long, we're going to get forgotten about and lose it all." Funnily enough, I think Ernie, who was very sensible, couldn't quite see that. He had stars in his eyes for Hollywood. Either way, they would have had an uphill struggle because they were so British, and Eric was not prepared to change things like lift to elevator and adopt all the various Americanisms.'

During Christmas 1962, Eric and Ernie returned to the Empire Liverpool, where they had first performed as a double act, to appear in Tom Arnold's production of *The Sleeping Beauty*. David Whitfield was once again top of the bill and the other cast members included Carol Layton, Dorothy Dampier and Eddie Molloy. The pantomime, which began on 21 December and ran until February 1963, was produced by Louis Barber and choreographed by Maureen Robbins.

A new series of thirteen thirty-minute editions of *The Morecambe and Wise Show* (*Two of a Kind*) began on 15 June 1963. For their third series for ATV, Eric and Ernie were obliged to record at ATV's studio complex at Borehamwood as the Wood Green Empire had ceased to be used by the company. This time, their guests included Joe Brown, the Mike Sammes Singers, Sheree Winton (mother of Dale Winton), the King Brothers, Barbara Law, Norman Mitchell, Roy Castle, Shani Wallis, Kathy Kirby and Rosemary Squires.

For the summer season in 1963, Morecambe and Wise appeared in *Show Time*, presented by Bernard Delfont at the North Pier Pavilion in Blackpool. The company also included Matt Monro, Russ Shepherd, and guest star Lena Martell, direct from her run of cabaret performances at the Pigalle Club in London's Piccadilly. The season began with a Gala Opening on 31 May at 7.30pm. Thereafter, performances were twice nightly at 6.00pm and 8.30pm.

On 22 November 1963, Eric and Ernie were presented with their first BAFTA award. While they were on stage, the tragic news filtered through the audience that President Kennedy had been assassinated.

At the end of 1963, the duo appeared in Tom Arnold and Bernard Delfont's production of *The Sleeping Beauty* at the Bristol Hippodrome. Eric played the King and Ernie played Presto, the Jester; and the cast also included Edmund Hockridge, Judy Clare, Eddie Molloy and Tessa Jarvis. The show ran from Christmas Eve until

March 1964 and broke all previous box office records for the theatre. To help spread the word, a special 'Mackeson' beer mat was produced to advertise the panto. Here is an extract from an article that the duo contributed to, reminding readers that they took beer-mat collecting very seriously:

> There is nothing half-soaked about beer-mat collecting. It's an interesting hobby and, as presidents of the Beer Mat Collectors Society (oh yes, it's come this far!), we would like to make it clear that the beer mat has now joined the matchbox label, beer bottle label, postage stamp, coin of the realm, bus ticket and cheese label, as a collector's item.
>
> With us, this hobby – respectably called tegestology – began as a joke, but we became so involved and inundated with beer mats of all kinds, that we genuinely began to take an interest in it.
>
> Then, in 1960, we were invited to become Honorary Joint Presidents of the first Beer Mat Collectors' society, and we gladly accepted.
>
> The object of the society is simple – to keep all beer mat collectors well informed about new issues and to arrange, when possible, meetings among members to discuss and to exchange specimens.
>
> We now have well over one thousand different kinds of mats from all over the world. And it may interest you to know that in Australia, beer mats are called 'coasters', while in the trade they are referred to as 'drip mats'. You now have our permission to call us Head Drips!

One evening during the panto, Morecambe and Wise decided to improvise their famous 'Boom Oo Yatta-Ta-Ta' routine. Equally of note is that it was during the run that Eric first became friends with Cary Grant, who had returned to his home town of Bristol for the festive season. Eric and Cary's friendship would last for twenty years; Eric's son would later co-write a book on Grant, called *Cary Grant: In Name Only*, with Martin Stirling.

On Valentine's Day 1964, Eric and Ernie attended the baptism of Eric's goddaughter, Leigh Miles, at the Church of St George the Martyr at Brandon Hill in Bristol. Jackie Hockridge, the wife of Edmund Hockridge who was appearing in pantomime with the double act in Bristol at the time, became Leigh's godmother. Leigh's mother is Maureen Robbins, and her father was Alex Myles. Both were good friends and colleagues of Morecambe and Wise. Leigh went on to become a professional dancer in 1979, appearing in a huge number of productions worldwide, but predominantly worked as one of Britain's top television dancers. She performed in many pantomimes and was one of the presenters on the BBC's popular children's series *Crackerjack*.

On Wednesday 19 February 1964, the *Daily Mirror* newspaper printed an article explaining Eric and Ernie's interest in helping to buy the film company, British Lion.

Comedians Morecambe and Wise have joined the 'Who'll-buy-British-Lion?' bidding.

Ernie Wise (the dumpy one) said last night, 'I understand the cost would be £1,600,000.

'It seems a bit steep, but we plan to approach Ken Dodd, Harry Worth, Harry Secombe, May Bygraves and other entertainers to see if we can raise the money between us.

'If we succeed, we would hire a production unit to make television films for marketing abroad.'

Ernie, 38, added, 'Very few British comics have a chance to appear in films nowadays with the present state of the film industry.'

British Lion Films are being sold by the government-backed National Film Finance Corporation. Seven bids have been made so far.

Morecambe and Wise, now appearing in *The Sleeping Beauty* pantomime at Bristol, wrote to Mr Edward Heath, Minster for Industry, about buying British Lion more than a week ago. So far, they have had no reply.

Quite why the reporter, Ned Grant, felt the need to refer to Ernie as 'the dumpy one' is unknown. Either way, Morecambe and Wise's idea for forming a consortium to buy British Lion and make television films never materialised.

The Morecambe and Wise Show (*Two of a Kind*) began a run of thirteen thirty-five-minute editions on 4 April 1964. In an edition of the show taped on

2 December 1963, and first broadcast on 18 April 1964, The Beatles (jokingly referred to as the Kaye Sisters by Eric) made a memorable appearance. The warm-hearted banter exchanged in the sketch remains a pleasure to watch and is arguably one of the best moments from Morecambe and Wise's years at ATV. The laughs come thick and fast as Eric calls Ringo Starr 'Bongo' and then later 'Bonzo', Paul McCartney incorrectly remembers Eric as 'the one with short, fat hairy legs' and George Harrison quotes Eric's famous 'get out of that' catchphrase. However, John Lennon's exchange with Morecambe tops them all:

Eric: What's it like being famous?
John: Well, it's not like in your day, you know.
Eric: Ha! That was an insult, that! (to Ernie) You
         didn't expect that, did you?
Ernie: No!
Eric: What do you mean 'not like in my day'?
John: Well, me Dad used to tell me about you, you
         know. (John indicates with his hand how tall he
         was, when his Dad told him. Eric deliberately
         misunderstands.)
Eric: You've only got a little Dad, have you?

Dressed in a typical Beatles suit of the era, and sporting a wig with their iconic mop-top hairstyle, Eric then proceeds to shout out random lyrics from some of the group's records of the day while John, Paul, George, Ringo and Ernie, dressed in smart blazers and straw boater hats, perform a slightly adapted version of the song 'Moonlight Bay' by way of a finale to the programme.

Other guests who appeared during Morecambe and Wise's fourth series at ATV included Eddie Calvert and the 'C' Men, Jackie Trent, Edmund Hockridge, Kathy Kirby, Joe Brown and the Bruvvers, Dickie Valentine, the Bachelors, Alan Curtis and Ray Ellington.

Despite an incredibly busy schedule, Eric and Ernie found the time in May 1964 to see their friend Bruce Forsyth make his cabaret debut at the Talk of the Town in Leicester Square.

Summer season that year saw Morecambe and Wise appear in *Show Time 1964*, at the Wellington Pier Pavilion in Great Yarmouth. Supporting performers for the run included Bert Weedon, the first British guitarist to have a hit record in the UK singles chart.

Anglia Television's Newman Sanders interviewed Eric and Ernie on the Wellington Pier just days before the summer season started. The light-hearted interview featured the act's usually unfinished 'two old men in deckchairs' joke as a running gag. Here are some extracts from the interview to show what Sanders was up against:

Newman:	Do you prefer playing on a pier or appearing on the telly? What is your favourite?
Ernie:	We enjoy all the mediums.
Eric:	All the mediums. And we're very medium in all of them. Aren't we?
Ernie:	Yes.

Eric also explained the origin of his second name:

Eric:	My name's Morecambe, you know.
Newman:	I know. Do you come from Morecambe?
Eric:	Yes, that's where I get the name from. Real name's Blackpool, but I never tell anybody, do I?

In a rare serious moment in the interview, Ernie revealed that this was the the duo's first summer season at Great Yarmouth, having only performed there in one week's variety prior to this. Other visits to the resort were to follow, however. Ernie also revealed that as he was living in Peterborough, he would be able to pop home to tend to his garden during the summer.

Eric's daughter, Gail, has happy memories of her childhood summer holidays and once described them as 'absolute bliss'. Both she and her brother, Gary, used to go and stay wherever Morecambe and Wise were appearing in summer season. While they were in Great Yarmouth, Gail would go to the theatre in the daytime with her father to pick up the post. 'I used to sit out front at the theatre and watch the show during the matinees,' she said. 'I used to get an overriding sense of joy from the audience and the special power Dad had over them. I recall that whenever he and Ernie went offstage the audience's shoulders would sort of slump down. It was as if they were waiting for the other acts to finish and for Dad and Ernie to come back on stage.'

Show Time 1964 played on the Wellington Pier twice nightly to capacity audiences. Eric and Ernie gave an example of the show's humour during a newspaper interview. During the performance, a straight man would pretend he was a late-arriving member of the audience:

> 'My seat's at the back,' says he, standing in the stalls.
> 'So's mine,' quips Morecambe from the stage.
> That's the kind of comedy the holidaymakers expect in a summer show, the pair explained. 'We wouldn't do this sort of stuff on television,' said Wise.
> 'Wouldn't we?' said Morecambe. 'Oh, I don't know…'

Somehow, in the same year, Eric and Ernie squeezed in the recording of a successful LP of songs and sketches, called *Mr Morecambe Meets Mr Wise*, at EMI's then Abbey Road Studios. They also managed to find time to pass judgement on other people's records when they appeared on an edition of *Juke Box Jury*, which was broadcast by the BBC at 5.15pm on 28 November 1964.

David Jacobs was in the chair and that week's panel also featured Lulu and Jean Metcalfe.

'The year 1964 bounded in leaving us breathless, intoxicated,' explained Eric in an interview in 1973. 'Whatever we touched turned to gold, or so people said. Money was pouring in, but wasn't that what we had been striving for all these years? Who could complain? Only it seemed the trouble with making big money is that it becomes a terrible habit. You can't refuse a good offer – after the tough early times you've been through, you hate turning anything down. Indeed, your conditioned reflexes make it impossible. You have become like Pavlov's dogs, except that, instead of salivating when the bell rings, your hand goes involuntarily into the signing twitch.'

By now, the Morecambe family had moved into a bigger home in Harpenden, Hertfordshire. Although Eric would live in this house for the rest of his life, he would continue to make trips to his home town of Morecambe – and not just for family reasons. Because he never forgot his roots, the comedian was held in high regard by locals. The return journey to Harpenden always saw his car boot filled to the brim with Morecambe Bay shrimps, sticks of Morecambe rock and fistfuls of crab claws.

Despite all their success, there was one medium Morecambe and Wise had yet to tackle at this stage in their careers. Despite an increasingly heavy workload, this was about to change.

5

Pinewood Bound

TELEVISION HAD MADE THE comedians the
hottest box-office proposition in the country.
This prompted Eric to explain to a journalist,
'And that's why we're not going back yet. We are giving
it a rest while they still like us. We're not fools.' Ernie
was in total agreement. 'We don't want to do too much.
Right now, we're at the peak, but you've got to make it
last as long as you can. You can't last for ever and we
haven't always been so lucky on television.'

In late 1964, Eric and Ernie motored to Pinewood
Studios in leafy Buckinghamshire to begin shooting *The
Intelligence Men*, the first of three feature films for The
Rank Organisation. The film was scripted by their ATV

writers, Sid Green and Dick Hills, and directed by Robert Asher, who also helmed certain episodes of the action television dramas *The Avengers*, *The Saint* and *The Champions*. The producer was Hugh Stewart, a former film editor whose other credits for Rank included producing nine of Norman Wisdom's films. Appearing alongside Eric and Ernie were an impressive cast including William Franklyn, April Olrich, Gloria Paul, Richard Vernon, David Lodge, Terence Alexander, Francis Matthews, Warren Mitchell and Brian Oulton.

In the film, Eric played café owner Eric Morecambe, and Ernie played a civil service pen-pusher, Ernie Sage. In the story, both men end up as MI5 spies after Eric discovers the existence of an international criminal gang. Our two heroes then help to foil an assassination attempt upon a Russian ballerina during a performance of *Swan Lake* at Covent Garden.

Sadly, the critic Leslie Halliwell was straight to the point in his review of the film, calling it an 'inept and rather embarrassing big-screen debut for two excellent television comedians'. Ironically, the film was one of the twelve most popular movies at the British box office when it was originally released in 1965!

Asked in 1966 about the difficulties of making a film, Eric and Ernie explained the problems of trying to establish whether a scene worked or not. Not having an audience, they had originally tried to gauge the reaction of the film crew; but, being used to the cumulative laughter of several hundred people throughout a whole show, to suddenly find themselves only performing for a minute at a time to a handful of crew members in a large sound stage was slightly unnerving. And while you could be forgiven for thinking that viewing the daily rushes would have put them at ease, this was not the case. Eric once claimed they were both 'frightened to death' of the rushes, so much so that, in the end, they stopped going to the preview theatre. One of Ernie's biggest frustrations with the films, he claimed, was that once the film was finished and being shown in the cinemas, it couldn't be changed.

Morecambe and Wise appeared in their third (and, as it turned out, final) Royal Command Performance on 2 November 1964. Presented by Bernard Delfont, the show was staged at The London Palladium and held in the presence of Queen Elizabeth II. The cast also included the Tiller Girls, Tommy Cooper, the Bachelors, Gil Dova, Cilla Black, Millicent Martin, Kathy Kirby, Brenda Lee, Dennis Spicer, Gracie Fields, the Moiseyev Dance Company, Ralph Reader's Gang Show, Jimmy Tarbuck, Cliff Richard and the Shadows, Bob Newhart, and Lena Horne with the Chico Hamilton Quartette.

It was Jimmy Tarbuck's first ever Royal Command Performance, and he had the honour of sharing a dressing room with Eric and Ernie, Tommy Cooper, and ventriloquist Dennis Spicer. While Eric and Ernie were rehearsing on stage, Tommy Cooper unplugged the dressing-room phone and locked it in a cupboard. This rather shocked the young comedian. 'I was still very much a boy in those days, and may have looked a little bit surprised,' admitted Jimmy. 'Tommy gave his confidential cough, and explained. "You've got to watch these pros," he said. "While I'm on stage, they'll be phoning Hong Kong."

'Then it was Tommy's turn to rehearse, and Eric and Ernie came back to the dressing room. Eric was on it in no time. "Now then, sunshine," said Eric. "Where's the phone?" "Tommy locked it in the cupboard," I replied. "He said you'd be phoning Hong Kong." We had a laugh about it, then a few hours later we were all in the dressing room waiting for the Queen to arrive. Suddenly, just down the corridor, the stage-door telephone started ringing. Eric had the answer. "Tommy," he said. "It's long-distance in the cupboard!" Well, I just couldn't stop laughing!'

Equally memorable for Jimmy is an act of kindness which Eric made to his fellow comedian that evening. 'I was in the second half of the show. The others had been on, but I will never forget that Eric came down specially to wish me luck before I went on stage. It was typical of the man that he wanted to encourage a young fellow-comedian, and I have since tried to do the same for young comedians.'

At the end of 1964, the tall one with the glasses and the short one with the fat hairy legs appeared in *The Sleeping Beauty* at the Palace Theatre, Manchester. The pantomime had a box office advance of one hundred thousand pounds. Edmund Hockridge, Eddie Molloy and Dorothy Dampier all shared the stage with Eric and Ernie. The only downside to the run was that prior to one performance, Ernie accidentally swallowed a front tooth!

On Tuesday 9 March 1965, Morecambe and Wise attended the Variety Club of Great Britain Awards Luncheon for 1964 at the Savoy Hotel in London. Eric and Ernie were declared 'Show Business Personalities' of the year during the ceremony, hosted by Peter Haigh. Edited highlights of the awards were broadcast by the BBC at 11.00pm that evening.

Eric and Ernie's 1965 summer season was staged at the ABC Theatre in Blackpool. The twice-nightly show at 6.10pm and 8.45pm was presented by Leslie Grade and Bernard Delfont in association with ABC. Appropriately it went by the name of *The Morecambe and Wise Show*. The company also featured Anna Dawson, Mark Wynter, Three Hermanis, Marvo and Delores, the Alfrero and the Pamela Devis Dancers. During the run, Barry Cryer visited Eric and Ernie backstage. 'I was standing in the wings and saw them rush off stage after receiving enormous applause,' he said. 'Eric's dresser was waiting with a lit cigarette. Eric had a quick drag before running back on stage for the finale; it was an energy-sapping performance.'

In 1965, it was back to Pinewood Studios for Morecambe and Wise to make, arguably, the best of their three Rank Organisation films, *That Riviera Touch*. Written by Sid Green and Dick Hills with Peter Blackmore, the film, which was released the following year, was directed by Cliff Owen and produced by Hugh Stewart. Suzanne Lloyd, Paul Stassino, Armand Mestral, Gerald Lawson, George Eugeniou, George Pastell, Alexandra Bastedo, Nicole Shelby, Peter Jeffrey, Francis Matthews, Michael Forrest and Paul Danquah were just some of the film's supporting cast.

Eric and Ernie played traffic wardens Eric Simpson and Ernie Clark. After Eric attempts to give a parking ticket to Her Majesty's car, the two men decide to resign and head for a holiday in the south of France. Once there, they find themselves being used by jewel thief Le Pirate (Paul Stassino) to aid his criminal activities. Along the way, Eric accidentally wins a large amount of money at a casino and the two innocents abroad become attracted to one of Le Pirate's gang, Claudette (Suzanne Lloyd). Additionally, Ernie falls in love with Eric's money. Somehow Eric and Ernie, who soon become aware of the criminal intrigue that surrounds them, manage to help the French police catch Le Pirate.

Due to her previous credits, actress Suzanne Lloyd didn't have to audition for the role of Claudette. In fact, she didn't get to meet Morecambe and Wise until they were all aboard a plane bound for the south of France. While on location, Eric and Ernie and their wives found themselves socialising with actors Tony Curtis and Omar Sharif, who were also filming on the French Riviera at the same time. Not surprisingly, this proved to be one of the biggest highlights of making the film. 'A group of Americans were also filming there, and we all used to take dinner together in this French café,' remembered Eric's wife, Joan. 'Some of the happiest days of our lives were spent over there.'

Eric and Ernie had by now spent sixteen consecutive Christmases working away from home in pantomime. As they explained to journalist Jilly Bury in late 1965, depending on the weather, they always tried to get to their respective homes for Christmas; but even then, they had to be back for the Boxing Day matinee. And given their schedules, it wasn't always possible to completely switch off and relax, as the interview proved:

> Ernie: We were often learning our parts on Christmas Day, since we only had about two days' rehearsal before opening. Sometimes we couldn't remember a word.

Eric: We would tag on to anyone in the cast who happened to live near the theatre and was having a party on Christmas Day.

Ernie: Occasionally we visited an old people's home or hospital. We would sit and talk to them…

Eric: And pinch all the fruit. We have had some good Christmases, but nothing's really the same as being at home with the family.

Eric and his wife, Joan, have two children – Gail, twelve, and Gary, nine. Did he phone home on Christmas Day?

Eric: You must be joking – it costs double on Christmas Day! I did ring them, of course. And the kids would tell me all about their presents. Joan always used to leave the decorations up for weeks after Christmas, so that when I got home, we could have a family party again and I could open my presents.

This year, things will be quite different for Eric and Ernie. They have just finished making their second film, *That Riviera Touch*, and in the New Year they start work on a new television series. Christmas 1965 will be a complete holiday for both of them.

Ernie plans to spend a quiet Christmas with his wife, Doreen, and her parents.

Eric: Counting last year's takings.

Ernie: I mean to have the first slice of the breast of the turkey. There's really nothing the same as home cooking.

> Edmund Hockridge, who lives next door, will probably
> join Ernie and his wife for part of Christmas.
>
> Eric: Ernie will go into the garden and sing 'Hey There'
>   over the back fence.
>
> Eric, Joan and the children will have a party at home,
> with the grandparents. The Morecambes and the Wises
> won't see anything of each other over Christmas 1965.

Eric and Ernie were quick to point out at the end of the interview that the reason was that being in each's pockets for three hundred and sixty-four days of the year was more than enough!

Sadly, Ernie's father, Harry, passed away on 18 February 1966. Despite this devastating start, the year would prove to be a busy and successful one for both Morecambe and Wise. As there had been no new editions of *The Morecambe and Wise Show* (*Two of a Kind*) in 1965, a new series of nine thirty-five-minute editions began on 29 January 1966. The guests taking part included Lulu, Wanda Ventham, Susan Maughan, Jackie Trent, Ann Hamilton, Georgie Fame, Barbara Law, The Shadows, Herman's Hermits and Pearl Carr and Teddy Johnson. Eric and Ernie's fifth series for ATV marked Ann Hamilton's first appearance on television with Morecambe and Wise. Her first sketch, in which Eric spends most of the time attempting to make passes at Hamilton, was a send up of *The Man from U.N.C.L.E.*:

Ernie: We're the Men from U.N.C.L.E.

Eric turns to admire Ann Hamilton, who's standing next to him in a fetching costume, including a white top and black leather skirt.

Eric: The Men from U.N.C.L.E.? Is it Dick? Nah, it's not Dick. It's too soft for Dick. It's probably Sid.

About halfway into the sketch, Ann is suddenly unable to keep her straight face and laughs at the way Eric delivers a line. Fortunately, she was able to compose herself straight away, although she momentarily did the same later. Ann later revealed that she found a unique way of preventing this from happening again in the future. She would vanish to the solitude of her dressing room after the final rehearsal to run over her lines and pretend to herself that she hated Eric and Ernie. This stopped her from laughing during the radio or television recordings made in the presence of a studio audience. Although it may have appeared otherwise, keeping to the script was important. 'There were no ad-libs unless something went wrong,' said Ann.

Millicent Martin was also invited to guest-star in Morecambe and Wise's fifth series for ATV. She was a huge fan of the duo and wasted no time in agreeing to appear. One of the sketches she featured in involved a wall. The idea was that each of the men attempted to sing 'Moonlight Becomes You' with Millicent on their own. Ernie began to sing the song with her, before Eric pulled him backwards off the wall. Then Ernie climbed back up and did the same to Eric. This continued until eventually they both did the same to Millicent. During the take, she was pulled backwards, missed the mattress that had been placed there to break their falls, and hit the floor lamp at the back. Although the singer was not hurt, Eric and Ernie were upset at what had happened.

The memorable routine has been a staple of pantos for years. Although the song that is used changes, the routine tends to remain the same. Cannon and Ball repeated it on TVS's *Summertime Special* with Lulu during the 1980s; and, proving that good comedy doesn't date, Ant and Dec later performed the routine with Jess Glynne while she tried to sing 'Hold My Hand' on an edition of ITV's *Saturday Night Takeaway*.

By now, Pearl Carr and Teddy Johnson had been good friends with both Eric and Ernie for several years. Having regularly appeared with them on stage and television, it was no surprise when, beginning on 30 May 1966, they joined the double act when they topped the bill for a week's variety at Coventry Theatre. The cast also included Arthur Worsley and Eddie Calvert.

Eric and Ernie performed in two Sunday concerts in June that year – one at Bridlington and the other at Torquay. They then decamped to Bournemouth for a twice-nightly summer season at the Winter Gardens, called *Show of Stars*. The cast included Susan Maughan, Ivor Emmanuel, Eric Delaney and his Band, and ventriloquist Arthur Worsley with Charlie Brown. The show was produced by Jack Douglas's brother, Bill Roberton, and was choreographed by his wife, Rita King. Sketches and special material were by Sid Green and Dick Hills. During the seven-week run, the double act played to an enviable ninety-eight per cent capacity. Also appearing in the resort that summer were performers including Harry Worth, in *Here's Harry*, with Mike Yarwood and Billy Dainty, at the Pavilion Theatre; and Sidney James in the Sam Cree farce *Wedding Fever* at the Pier Theatre.

The summer of 1966 also saw Morecambe and Wise make a welcome return to radio when editions of *The Morecambe and* Wise Show were broadcast on the Light Programme. The boys were also Roy Plomley's guests on the long-running *Desert Island Discs* on Monday 29 August. The programme, which was produced by Michael Hall, was broadcast at 12.20pm and repeated the following Saturday at 1.40pm.

Eric and Ernie completed their contractual obligation with Rank by making *The Magnificent Two* at Pinewood Studios in 1966. The screenplay was written by Sid Green and Dick Hills with Michael Pertwee and Peter Blackmore. The film, which was released into cinemas the following year, was directed by Cliff Owen and produced by Hugh Stewart. Supporting Eric and

Ernie for their third attempt at silver-screen success were cast members including Margit Saad, Virgilio Teixeira, Cecil Parker, Isobel Black, Martin Benson, Tyler Butterworth (son of Peter Butterworth), Sandor Elès, Victor Maddern and Michael Gover. Eric and Ernie played a couple of down-on-their-luck salesmen who find themselves caught in the middle of a revolution in South America. Eric ends up pretending to be the late figurehead of the revolution, Fernando Torres, after his supporters discover that Eric is his double.

Eric's wife, Joan, was philosophical about the three cinema outings Morecambe and Wise made during the 1960s. 'I think the three Rank films Eric and Ernie did were very enjoyable. But one can't pretend that they were classics in any way – because they weren't. However, they're still shown on television now and they do have an audience. They're for people who don't want to be too critical and just sit back and enjoy them. They're just light, relaxing entertainment. It was a bit of a disappointment to Eric and Ernie at the time that it wasn't something a little bit more special.'

Gail, Eric's daughter, remains supportive of the three Rank titles. 'I thoroughly enjoy the films Dad made with Ernie,' she said. 'I can't criticise them when I watch them. My favourite is *That Riviera Touch*.'

Although their first three films hadn't exactly matched the high expectations the industry and the public had in equal measure, Eric and Ernie were sent a film screenplay in 1967 entitled *Mr Mercury*. Sadly, it didn't appeal to them and they duly rejected it.

In 1966, Morecambe and Wise were asked if they thought of themselves consciously as a team. Their replies arguably prove how they saw their partnership by this time. Ernie replied, 'Yes, except we call ourselves Eric Morecambe and Ernie Wise whereas before we used to call ourselves Morecambe and Wise.' When the interviewer asked why, Eric replied, 'It was comic and straight man, but now it's comic and comic. Or as some people say, straight man and straight man!'

Due to the success of their first LP in 1964, in 1966 the duo released *An Evening with Ernie Wise at Eric Morecambe's Place*. They then ended the year by appearing in *The Sleeping Beauty* at Birmingham Theatre (Birmingham Hippodrome). The cast also featured Eddie Molloy, Betty Emery, Dorothy Dampier, Patricia Bredin, Jimmy Lee, John Perrin, Kevin Scott and the Betty Fox Babes. Here's an extract of Morecambe and Wise's biography from the programme for this pantomime:

> Two of Britain's busiest and funniest comics, Eric Morecambe and Ernie Wise, are undoubtedly the top comedy act on the entertainment scene today – as proved when they were voted Top TV Light Entertainment Personalities for ATV's *The Morecambe and Wise Show*

and Show Business Personalities of the Year by the Variety Club of Great Britain.

Whether they are appearing before Royalty – as they have done with 'show-stealing' success – or on television, in their own hilarious weekly comedy series, these comics have a happy knack of raising the roof with laughter in a relaxed, homely way.

Guided by an astute agent, Mr Billy Marsh of the Bernard Delfont Organisation, Eric and Ernie have come a long way in show business since they first formed their partnership.

Experience has led them to try most forms of entertainment – records, television, stage, films and even circus – so that today they are skilled entertainers who can time an off-the-cuff remark as expertly as a scripted joke, and make it sound as funny or at least three times funnier. Their subtle humour, with the 'visual catchphrases' they have made famous through television (remember 'get out of that' and 'short, fat hairy legs'?) has led them to the pinnacle of their profession. And the simple fun they get out of a brown paper bag has audiences all over Britain and in America rolling in the aisles.

A TV Today began broadcasting in the Midlands on Monday 5 October 1964 as a twenty-minute daily magazine programme. So naturally it was they who filmed a report, first shown on 22 December 1966, of Morecambe and Wise handing over a giant Christmas pudding to the Lord Mayor of Birmingham. As the surviving archive footage of this event is silent, one can only guess the witty lines Eric would have come out with during this task!

On Boxing Day 1966, John Swallow's interview with Eric and Ernie about their appearance in *The Sleeping Beauty* was broadcast for the first time on *ATV Today*. A much-loved reporter who was well known for his light-hearted television news reports in the Midlands, John started on *ATV Today* and later worked for *Central News* when the Midlands' ITV franchise changed from ATV to Central (Independent) Television in 1982. His encounter with Eric and Ernie has been included as part of an award-winning DVD package called *From Headlines to 'Tight-Lines': The Story of ATV Today*. Here is a transcript of part of the interview:

John: Did you have a good Christmas dinner yesterday?

Eric: Beautiful. We had chips. Always have chips at Christmas. (Hugs John)

Ernie: He's getting very friendly now.

Eric: I like people. It's people I like.

Ernie: Turkey, turkey?

Eric: Who is?

Ernie: I'll tell you something about Christmas: people don't realise it's not very nice for the turkeys.

Eric: It's all right in July when they're walking about in the heat.

Ernie: On the farm…

Eric: Saying 'Oh what a lovely day.' Suddenly it's Christmas. (Eric makes a hand chop gesture).

> Ernie: How would you like to be hanging up starkers in
> the butchers?

On 24 February 1967, Eric and Ernie were among the stage and screen personalities present at the annual theatre service at Birmingham Cathedral. Surviving silent archive footage filmed by ATV shows both men looking relaxed and sitting in one of the pews in the congregation.

Summer season in 1967 saw Eric and Ernie back at Great Yarmouth again. *The Morecambe and Wise Show*, presented by Leslie Grade in association with ABC, was a record-breaking run staged at the ABC Regal, which has long since been demolished. Those supporting the boys included Ivor Emmanuel, David and Marianne Dalmour, Saveen assisted by Daisy May, Eric Delaney and his Band, and the Pamela Devis Dancers. As a reminder of just how things have changed since the show was staged, if you had purchased a souvenir programme during the run it would have cost you a mere one shilling (five pence)!

Michael Grade joined Billy Marsh's agency in 1966 as an apprentice and shared an office with Marsh. This meant he often got to meet Morecambe and Wise when they visited to discuss business. 'I got on well with them and they liked me,' he said. 'I would sit in on their meetings with Billy, and chat and laugh with them.

'It was a pleasure to see them work. I used to go to Borehamwood to see them recording their television shows for ATV, and see them in concerts, pantomimes and summer seasons.'

Michael's favourite Morecambe and Wise recollection is of seeing the double act in their second summer season in Great Yarmouth. This show saw the first outing for the ventriloquist's dummy, Charlie, which Eric would later use on stage and television in a routine inspired by Sandy Powell's own ventriloquist's act. Grade remembers witnessing Eric and Ernie's own version during the run. 'The routine originally ran to about four or five minutes. It was an absolute triumph; Eric was ad-libbing away and Ernie was on fire. They were on cloud nine afterwards. By the end of the season the routine lasted about fifteen minutes!'

Professionally the 1967 summer season was incredibly successful, but during the summer Eric started to experience health symptoms that would develop into something life-threatening the following year. At the time, he noted that he had a slight pain around the left side of his heart. Although he initially dismissed it in his diary as wind, he recorded that he had experienced it for four days. However, he continued to perform in the show.

The sixth and final series of *The Morecambe and Wise Show* (*Two of a Kind*) began a UK run of ten sixty-minute editions on 1 October 1967. The series was renamed *Piccadilly Palace* when it was shown in America. Although Colin Clews had directed all of Eric and Ernie's own shows for ATV since 1961, Philip Casson was brought in to direct this series. Up until now, all the duo's programmes for ATV had been made in black and white. However, despite colour cameras being used during the recording of the series, the shows were only broadcast in colour in America. ITV viewers had to settle for black-and-white broadcasts as colour transmissions had not yet commenced on the network. The guests taking part in this final ATV series included Millicent Martin (who appeared in each edition), Freddie and the Dreamers, the Small Faces, the Hollies, Tom Jones, Manfred Mann, Gene Pitney, the Dave Clark Five and Cliff Richard.

Eric's daughter, Gail, had a crush on Gene Pitney at the time. Knowing this, her father invited her along to ATV to watch the singer recording his appearance on the show. During a break in the recording, and in front of Pitney, the crew and the studio audience, Eric took it upon himself to announce, 'My daughter's in love with you.' Gail recalled what happened next: 'I think poor Mr Pitney said something like, "Oh that's nice." Then Dad said, "She's in the audience tonight, would you like to meet her? Stand up, Gail. Where are you?" Many thoughts flashed through my mind at this point, some of them murderous, but I decided it would be better to stand up quickly, smile and sit down again. Rows of heads turned to see where I was. Mr Pitney kindly said, "Oh, she's lovely," to which my father replied, "Yes, we call her sparrow legs." I was very self-conscious about my skinny legs and now I wished I'd worn trousers and hoped I wouldn't even have to meet Gene Pitney after the show!'

The following year, Millicent Martin, Pearl Carr and Teddy Johnson, the Schaller Brothers, Joe McBride, and Ray Alan and Lord Charles were just some of the performers who travelled with Eric and Ernie to Toronto in Canada to appear in *The London Palladium Show*. The production ran at the O'Keefe Centre for two weeks from 13 to 25 May. Two paragraphs from the souvenir brochure reveal the thinking behind the production:

> Difficult though it may be to believe, this is the first time that a Palladium show has ventured outside the hallowed walls of the English-speaking world's leading variety house, and O'Keefe Centre is proud to have been chosen for the distinction of offering this 'first'.
>
> Depending how things go during this fortnight's run, a Palladium visit might become an annual event. We hope so. We also hope that Messrs Morecambe and Wise, Millicent Martin and all the other good people you will see at this performance enjoy their stay in Toronto and that you will enjoy having had them here. The

logistics of moving a show of this size across the Atlantic for a single two-week engagement are staggering but may the headaches all be forgotten when the final curtain falls on Saturday, May 25.

In 1968, Morecambe and Wise were starting to grow restless at ATV. They felt that they needed to expand beyond the black-and-white thirty-minute shows that they had been making for Lew Grade. They also felt, quite rightly, that they should receive a pay rise given the ratings they were bringing ITV. It looked as if a change was on the horizon. As with many times in Eric and Ernie's careers, a series of events would take place over the coming months that would catapult them even higher up the showbiz ladder.

6

Back to Auntie

HE PHONE IN BILL COTTON Junior's office rang. He answered it and was greeted by the voice of Michael Grade. Grade, acting as Morecambe and Wise's agent at Billy Marsh's office, explained that the boys had not come to an agreement with Lew Grade, and asked if he would be interested in signing them to the BBC. Cotton didn't need asking twice. Having made a total of six series and sixty-seven editions of *The Morecambe and Wise Show* (*Two of a Kind*) for ATV, it was time for the double act to return to the BBC. Very soon, a three-year deal was agreed that gave Eric and Ernie a colour BBC Two series called, not surprisingly, *The Morecambe and Wise Show*. The deal also included the condition that Sid Green and Dick Hills would continue to write the shows.

Johnny Ammonds was sitting in the bar at BBC Television Centre one lunchtime. 'Bill Cotton walked up to me and said, "How do you fancy producing Morecambe and Wise?"' recalled Johnny. 'I said, "Can a duck swim? But Lew Grade's got them." He said, "No, I have."'

The first eight episodes of *The Morecambe and Wise Show* were taped at BBC Television Centre and began transmission on BBC Two on 2 September 1968. Eric and Ernie's guests on the first series included Sid Green, Dick Hills, Acker Bilk, Roy Budd, Bruce Forsyth, Kenny Ball, Ronnie Carroll, Edmund Hockridge, Michael Aspel and Matt Monro.

To date, of the eight episodes, editions one, three, four and eight are still missing. Edition six still survives in the archives but only in edited form. Edition two has been found and work is being done to restore the programme using a ground-breaking new technique. Experts have managed to scan parts of the old decaying film copy using X-rays, and then employed an algorithmic reconstruction method to digitally recreate the images. In 2018, a thirty-second piece of this restored footage was released to the public online by the BBC.

Meanwhile, editions five and seven were found by archive preservation expert Philip Morris in excellent condition in an archive in Freetown, Sierra Leone. The sketches included 'Old Donegal', 'Instant Camera', 'Sailing Around the World', 'Eric and the Pools' and 'Hollywood Musical'. These were finally broadcast again by the BBC during Christmas 2018 – fifty years since they had first been seen by viewers. As Michael Aspel was in edition seven, he was given the honour of introducing the programmes.

In the autumn of 1968, Eric and Ernie agreed to journey back home to the north of England to begin a host of club bookings. The planned dates included a two-week run at the famous Batley Variety Club. On 8 November, Eric began to feel unwell. At around half past one in the morning, after the late-night show, the comedian began to drive back to his hotel in his Jensen. Sensing he was going to need help getting to hospital, Eric stopped a man in Leeds called Walter Butterworth who was on his way home from a night out. After a brief exchange of words, Walter, who was then a member of the Territorial Army, agreed to drive Eric to hospital – despite having only driven a tank before!

Eventually Eric was admitted to Leeds Infirmary. Despite lying there on a stretcher, and feeling very ill, Eric still managed to find the energy to thank Walter Butterworth for all his help. 'Oh, that's all right, it's a pleasure,' he replied. Walter then paused before delivering the now legendary words, 'My mates won't believe this. Will you do us a favour? Before you go, will you sign this?'

Back in their Harpenden home, Eric's wife, Joan, had just retired for the night when the phone rang. It was the hospital, who informed her that her husband had suffered a serious heart attack. They advised her that she travel up to Leeds as soon as possible. At that stage, they believed Eric would not recover.

'I think when Eric had his first major heart attack, which was very severe but was played down a lot, I think he felt then that he'd wanted to go back to work in show business,' recalled Joan. 'But he was going to give it a lot of time. He went back sooner than he intended because he was so well. But he intended to look after himself. He had no desire to take a short cut back to work. Eric was a nervous smoker with cigarettes, but he gave it up when he had a heart attack and never smoked another cigarette. His pipe was a dummy, in a way. His pipes got chewed on and the stems used to go. He did like to fill his pipe and have a smoke, although Eric wasn't much of a smoker in the end.'

Morecambe and Wise's spot at Batley Variety Club was taken over by the comedian Ted Rogers (who later became best known for hosting the gameshow *3-2-1!* on ITV) and Joan Turner. Meanwhile, the organisers of that year's Royal Command Performance had to decide who could take over Morecambe and Wise's planned appearance. In a rare interview, Mike Yarwood discussed how he came to be one of the stand-ins for the boys. 'I was not down to do this show, but Eric had a heart attack, and I happened to be at The London Palladium,' he remembered. 'Eric and Ernie were doing two spots in the show, and as stand-ins Frankie Howerd took one and I did the other. My greatest thrill was that I was in the number one dressing room, because it's theatrically ethical that if you replace a performer you naturally go into his room. I wasn't the senior star in the show, but I was in the star's dressing room, which was nice. I shared it with Engelbert Humperdinck, Des O'Connor and Frankie Howerd, but that was not a hardship. I just felt honoured being in that room which I had only visited before.'

Following Eric's heart attack, Ernie was interviewed by the *Yorkshire Evening Post*. At that time, no one knew who the mystery Samaritan was who helped to save his comedy partner's life. Wise told the newspaper, 'I don't know who the man is, but I would like to thank him. It was very good of him.' It wasn't long before clues to Walter Butterworth's identity were revealed in an interview included in the same newspaper article:

The clue to the man's identity came from Mr George Wood, a taxi proprietor of Lulworth Close, Whitkirk,

who took the man home after Mr Morecambe had been
taken to hospital.

He said, 'The man was aged between twenty-five and
thirty. He was slightly built and had sharp features.' Mr
Wood added, 'The man told me he was walking near
Leeds Parish Church when a car pulled up. The driver
asked if he knew where the nearest hospital was as he was
in pain.'

'The driver then asked if the man could drive and he
drove Mr Morecambe to the Infirmary. He must have
gone inside the hospital but did not leave his name.'

Mr Wood said the man then walked down to the taxi
rank in Quebec Street. 'I dropped him off at Thwaite
Gate, near the Red Lion. He must live nearby.'

Ernie explained Morecambe's condition during his
interview for the same newspaper. 'I have seen Eric in
hospital, and I think it is going to be about three months
before the act gets going again,' he said.

While he was recovering from his heart attack, Eric
discovered that Des O'Connor had told the audience of
his show in Paignton that Morecambe was fighting for
his life in hospital and, if they believed in such things,
to pray for his recovery. His reply was as witty as ever:
'Tell him that those six or seven people made all the
difference.'

Christmas 1968 would have been very different for
Eric and Ernie had the former been in better health.
Negotiations had taken place for them both to star in

that year's Christmas show at the Alhambra Theatre in Glasgow. A newspaper article printed that year reveals the original plans:

Howard and Wyndham Capture Morecambe and Wise

After months of negotiation, Howard and Wyndham have 'scooped the pool' and have great pleasure in announcing that Morecambe and Wise will be stars of this year's Christmas show at the Alhambra Theatre, Glasgow.

Eric and Ernie, Britain's top comedy team, are today not only the most sought-after comedians in Britain, but also in America. At present, they are regularly seen commuting between London and New York, for guest-star appearances in America's top television shows.

Opening on Friday, December 6, *The Morecambe and Wise Show* will run for an eight-week season. This will be the first time the two boys have appeared at the Alhambra Theatre.

Heading the supporting cast will be Moira Anderson, who since her last appearance at the Alhambra with Frankie Vaughan has, through the medium of television, become a star in her own right. Completing Dick Hurran's holiday spectacular will be a host of International Speciality Acts new to Glasgow audiences.

The Gala Opening will be at 7.30pm, thereafter twice nightly.

While he was convalescing, Eric relaxed by taking up birdwatching. This was a hobby he grew to love and would remain an important part of his life away from work. Speaking of hobbies, Eric acquired an impressive collection of Meerschaum pipes, featuring hand-carved likenesses of naked women, kings' heads, and even one shaped like a mermaid. But his real passion was for pocket watches; he is said, at the peak of his collecting, to have owned around fifty.

Morecambe and Wise's first stage appearance after Eric's heart attack was at the Pavilion Theatre, Bournemouth, in 1969. Their entrance onto the stage was greeted with a five-minute standing ovation. This reminded the boys of just how much they were still loved by the public.

Eric and Ernie decided they would now take longer over making their programmes in order to give proper consideration to the former's health. 'Bill Cotton Junior at the BBC was lovely,' said Eric's wife, Joan. 'He was always on their side and arranged that they could have extra rehearsal time, so they weren't running to such a tight schedule. That made a lot of difference to Eric, particularly with the Christmas shows. But they still had to do all the energetic dance routines because it was sort of expected of them.'

Although Eric had concerns about returning to work, his daughter, Gail, summarised how outwardly the situation looked to his colleagues. 'The second he got back to working, no one else would have known he'd had a heart attack,' she said.

There was one major problem that needed to be ironed out before the recording of a new series could commence: a new writer or writers had to be found, as Hills and Green were to return to working for ATV. In a moment of inspiration, Bill Cotton suggested that Eddie Braben would make a good principal writer for Eric and Ernie's future shows at the BBC.

Eddie was born in Liverpool in 1930. He grew up being fascinated by radio comedy, but left school with no real career plan in mind. 'I was an assistant to a bricklayer or, if you like, a brickie's labourer,' Eddie said. 'I had no idea what I wanted to do. So, in sheer desperation, my father bought me a little fruit-and-vegetable stall in what used to be St John's Market. But I didn't like it, I wasn't happy there.'

Braben was fast developing a sense of humour around this time. This led to him trying his hand at writing comedy in the evenings. But what started as a hobby soon became an obsession. 'I was doing it when I should have been selling the fruit,' he recalled. 'I was behind the stall writing down what I thought were funny things on little scraps of paper. I can honestly say that I used to write about three thousand jokes a week. And they were three thousand of the worst jokes you ever read in your life.'

Having sold his first joke to Charlie Chester for two shillings and sixpence, Eddie went on to write material for the Liverpool comedian Ken Dodd. However, Eddie and Ken had gone their separate ways by the time the vacancy arose for a new scriptwriter for Morecambe and Wise. 'When Bill Cotton said there was a chance that we might be able to get him, the boys said "great",' producer and director Johnny Ammonds revealed many years later. A meeting at BBC Television Centre ended with Eddie promising he would return in one week's time with material for Eric and Ernie and Cotton to read. A busy week ensued as the writer crafted a script which, he hoped, would convince them that his ideas, as different as they were to anything they had performed before, had potential.

The script reading at the return meeting brought laughter to the room, but Eric and Ernie weren't convinced that Eddie's material and proposed format for their future shows was quite them. Bill Cotton disagreed, and suggested they go ahead and record a single show featuring a script penned by Eddie. In other words, Eddie was being given an on-the-job audition. There was no promise that he would be given the chance to write any further editions of the show; on the contrary, it was made clear that Eric and Ernie would have to be convinced that he was right for the position.

Eddie Braben hadn't liked Morecambe and Wise's previous stage personas. 'Eric was too gormless, in my view,' he said. 'Ernie was too abrasive and hard-edged.

Yet, at that meeting it was obvious there was genuine friendship and affection between them. There was humility and innocence, too. None of that was being shown in their work, so I reckoned if all that could be developed, it would show a different, softer side to Morecambe and Wise.

'I came back with thirty pages of material with my vision of a new, reinvented Eric and Ernie,' remembered Eddie. 'In a way, I was caricaturing the two men as they really were. I never told Eric and Ernie that this was really a showcase for their mutual affection, because I was afraid they might become self-conscious and spoil it. Ernie was delighted with his new role. "At last I've got something to perform," he told me.'

Despite everyone being determined that Eric's stress levels should be kept low in order to protect his health, the first show back was anything but stress-free. There was a lot at stake. After all, this was Morecambe and Wise's first television show since Eric's heart attack. Everyone, including Eric, wondered if he would cope with the rigours of being back in a television studio. Throw in the worry of having a new writer, and you have the recipe for sleepless nights – for all concerned! It was a gamble, but fortunately it was a gamble that paid off. The recording was a success, Eric coped admirably and Braben was commissioned to work on the rest of the second series.

Eric was the first to admit that the process of writing the scripts for *The Morecambe and Wise Show* was always going to be an uphill struggle. 'He's got the worst job in the world, hasn't he?' Morecambe once pointed out. 'He's got his own house, with his own little office, and he goes in there on a Monday morning with a typewriter and a blank sheet of paper. And then he starts from there. And that's it, that's the hard bit.

'Eddie thinks of things that we think are very funny, and I wish to God we could think of. But we can't.'

Braben himself would later reveal how the increasing popularity of the shows would play on his mind. 'The real pressure came when I was sat in front of that typewriter with all those blank pages and there was a deadline and there was nothing happening. That's when you realised there were twenty million or twenty-five million people looking over your shoulder, all saying "make me laugh".'

Eric and Ernie had a great affection for Braben, but for a while there was one sticking point – the bed sketches. Given how well remembered and loved they have remained, it's hard to believe there was a time when the double act weren't keen on the idea. In a fit of frustration, Eddie managed to convince the two men that they should include them in their shows. How? He argued that if bed scenes were good enough for Laurel and Hardy in their films, then they were good enough for Morecambe and Wise. They agreed, and from then on bedroom sketches became a regular feature of their programmes.

It's interesting to note that the writers Ray Galton and Alan Simpson, who famously wrote *Hancock's Half Hour* and *Steptoe and Son*, once jointly expressed how they wished they had worked for both men, and their admiration for Eddie Braben. 'During our long and varied career, we had the pleasure of working with most of the top-line comedians in the business, some of whom actually survived the experience. The one notable exception was Morecambe and Wise, whom we never wrote for, something we always regretted, they being one of the few double acts who were worth twice as much money as the best solo acts. In fact, they were really a treble act. We must never forget their writer, the superb Eddie Braben.'

Speaking about the rehearsal period for the BBC programmes, Eric said, 'We start at, say, ten or half past ten and we finish at between three and half past three. But we go straight through, we don't stop for lunch or anything.'

Eric's wife, Joan, has clear memories of how making the programmes affected her husband. 'When Eric had taped a television show, he could never just switch off afterwards,' she said. 'He had to stay behind at the studio and have chats with people who had been taking part in the show. Ernie would dash off with Doreen, but Eric would always stay behind for at least an hour.

'I always used to go to the actual recordings and thoroughly enjoyed it, of course. Eric didn't want me around at the rehearsals. In fact, he didn't want anyone around other than the people concerned. But he did like to see my reaction and for me to be there for the actual show. And, come what may, I always went to all the BBC shows. I don't think I ever missed one. It's a long while ago, but I recall that I attended as many of their radio shows as I could.

'After an hour or so after a television recording, Eric would come home, but he would never go to bed straight away. He would usually have a meal then, as invariably he hadn't eaten. He'd have supper and he'd just sit and talk, or if the telly was still on, he'd watch it a bit before he finally went to bed.'

Mike Fountain had a successful car-hire firm in Harpenden during the late 1960s. He had a contract with the BBC to take Eric to and from rehearsals and recordings. After the contract ended, Eric asked Mike if he would like a full-time job as his chauffeur. After just a few seconds, Mike replied, 'Yes, please, I'll take the job.' From then he was the comedian's chauffeur right up until his untimely death in 1984. He has often stated in interviews that the days he worked with Eric were the happiest of his life.

Series two began on 27 July 1969, with the last of the four fortnightly editions going out on 7 September. The guests in the series included Peter Cushing, Bobbie Gentry, Vince Hill, Kenny Ball and his Jazzmen, Juliet Mills, Moira Anderson, Edward Woodward, Kenneth McKellar, Janet Webb and Ann Hamilton. Highlights of the series included Peter Cushing playing the role of King Arthur in Ernie Wise's first ever play 'wot he wrote', called *Knights of the Round Table*. This saw the start of a long-running gag in which Cushing kept asking to be paid for his initial appearance. The veteran actor also appeared in the fourth edition, in which he and Edward Woodward starred in Ernie's play *Murder at the Grange*. During the spoof, a distressed Woodward asked Peter why he hadn't warned him what it would be like working with Eric and Ernie.

The series, now in its forty-five-minute format, also saw Morecambe and Wise perform 'Bring Me Sunshine', written in 1966 by composer Arthur Kent with lyrics by Sylvia Dee, on television for the first time. The skip-dance that would become synonymous with this song when it was performed by Eric and Ernie was chosen thanks to the series' producer and director, Johnny Ammonds. 'I saw Groucho Marx in a film called *Horse Feathers*, and at one point he did a silly dance. I did it round the rehearsal hall, because it was just Eric and Ernie there, nobody else, and they collapsed on the floor when I did it. And they did it after "Bring Me Sunshine" and it became a trademark.'

Eric accepted an invitation to be a guest on the BBC Radio 4 programme *What Did You Do in the War, Daddy?* in 1969. This featured the story of the men who spent World War Two down the mines. It thus gave Eric the opportunity to discuss the spell he spent working as a Bevin Boy. The programme was originally broadcast on 19 September 1969.

That year heralded the arrival of one of the most important aspects of Morecambe and Wise's television career – the first of their legendary Christmas shows. Broadcast on Christmas Day, Eric and Ernie's guests were Frankie Vaughan, Nina, the Pattersons, Fenella Fielding, Sacha Distel, Alan Curtis and Diane Keen. Although Diane Keen would be given guest star billing with the boys on an edition of their television show in 1981, her appearance at the start of this Christmas special was a rather more modest one. Diane laughed when she was reminded that her character name was 'Dolly Bird'. She can still clearly remember the outfit she wore on the show. 'I wore a curly blonde wig and a black minidress,' she said. During the sketch, Ernie, dressed in a trendy outfit of the era, attempts to persuade Eric that he must dress like him if he wants to attract 'the birds'. Diane then enters and, despite appearing to be impressed with little Ern, walks off with the tall one with the glasses. 'The sketch was a lot of fun,' said Diane. 'Eric kept making faces at my awful wig, which of course made me want to laugh.'

There used to be a one-armed car-park attendant called George who worked at BBC Television Centre. George had his favourite performers and staff members. This meant some people would get a parking place and others did not. One day, George asked Eric if there was any chance of him getting tickets for a Christmas show they were about to record. 'No,' Eric replied. George was shocked and said, 'Why?' 'What would be the point?' replied Eric. 'You've only got one arm and you won't be able to clap!' Just in case you were wondering, George did get his tickets!

Viewers didn't have to wait long for their next fix of Eric and Ernie. Their third series of *The Morecambe and Wise Show*, consisting of seven editions, began on 14 January 1970. As with series two, the programmes were shown fortnightly; guests included Herman's Hermits, Jimmy Clitheroe, Jenny Lee-Wright, Clodagh Rodgers, Kenny Ball and his Jazzmen, Sacha Distel, Diane Cilento, Vince Hill, Deryck Guyler, Frank Thornton, Nina, Richard Greene, Nana Mouskouri and the Athenians, Ann Hamilton and Janet Webb. Edition three of this series featured a re-edited version of the 1969 Christmas show with the addition of new material. But while six editions of the series lasted forty-five minutes in length, edition six, which was taped and entered for the Golden Rose of Montreux, the prestigious international awards festival in entertainment broadcasting, ran at just thirty minutes. The same edition featured a sketch in which Eric and Ernie attempt to swap trousers. Although the rest of the edition was written by Eddie Braben, this sketch was one that Hills and Green had penned for the double act during their ATV days.

Even though Eric and Ernie's film career had somewhat stalled after *The Magnificent Two*, a short sound-effect comedy film called *Simon Simon*, released in 1971, did at least give them a chance to dabble in the medium again – even if they only had cameo roles! Eric played a roofer and Ernie a painter and decorator. The film featured Graham Stark and John Junkin as two workmen; and the cast also included Julia Foster, Norman Rossington, Peter Sellers, Michael Caine, Tommy Godfrey, Bob Monkhouse and Tony Blackburn. The production was written and directed by Graham Stark, with additional material provided by Dave Freeman.

Eric's devotion to the pipe resulted in him being voted 'Pipe Smoker of the Year' in 1970. The year also saw him becoming a director of Luton Town FC. Roger Wash, an official club historian, vividly remembers Eric's association with the football club. 'Eric started to watch Luton in the late 1960s, to try and indoctrinate his son Gary to the game,' said Roger. 'The Luton secretary at the time made sure that Eric's seat was next to the directors' box, leading to him being asked to the board-room for drinks after each game. This, in turn, led to him becoming a director of the club. With Morecambe and Wise's shows playing to huge audiences, and the "Hatters" doing well on the pitch, it was a marriage made in heaven. Eric mentioning his beloved football team at every opportunity was the best PR a club could wish for.

'Although Eric took his director role at the club very seriously, he obviously loved an audience and played up to the cameras whenever possible. In those days, the club used to charter special trains to away games for the princely sum of 25 shillings (£1.25); and, wherever we went, the players and officials took up a couple of carriages as well. My abiding memory is of Eric walking up and down the corridors chatting to the supporters, practising his paper bag trick, adjusting people's glasses and generally acting the fool for hours on end. Eric was a genuinely nice man and a natural comedian as well.'

Another long-time admirer of Luton Town FC is the broadcaster Nick Owen. 'I am not sure when I first became aware of Eric Morecambe – it was probably during my teenage years – but it is fair to say he has been my hero for decades,' he recalled. 'As in many households, watching Eric and Ernie was always a family event for my parents and me. I loved their shows, but my enthusiasm positively rocketed when Eric started to support my beloved Luton Town FC because he had set up home just down the road in Harpenden. The buzz that went around the ground when he took his seat at Kenilworth Road was something really special. He later became a director and raised the club's profile enormously. A number of clips in Eric and Ernie's shows feature Luton and it still gives me a tingle when I see them now.

'Because of my job as a broadcaster, I was lucky enough to meet and interview Eric a couple of times. The first was when I was a local radio sports presenter with BBC Radio Birmingham in the seventies. The programmes came from the BBC's Pebble Mill studios; and, one Christmas, Eric and Ernie were there recording a show for television. We persuaded Eric to come to the radio studio where I was hosting a four-hour (mainly football) show, and we chatted on air for about an hour between live reports from elsewhere. He was an absolute joy, cracking jokes and, much to my delight, raving on about Luton legends such as Malcolm Macdonald.'

Fellow double act Cannon and Ball were invited to appear at a charity event hosted at Luton FC. Bobby Ball still remembers the thrill they both had on meeting Eric at the ground. 'Tommy and I were great fans of Eric and Ernie's, and one of the biggest highs of our career was when we were invited to Luton Town FC to visit some children and Eric happened to be there. To meet one of our heroes, well, one can't explain the feeling. He greeted us and told us he was a great admirer of our comedy, which once again blew our minds away.

'We went to meet the children, who were all having fizzy drinks. At that time, Tom and I were flying with our own television series every Saturday night on ITV, so this was my chance to show off in front of Eric! Lifting myself up to my full height (five feet four inches), I pulled my braces and shouted at the top of my voice, "Rock on Tommy!" There was silence: not a murmur. The kids just looked at me with open mouths! Then Eric stepped forward and said, "No, this is how you do it Bobby," and he put his glasses to one side of his face, how he used to do, and shouted, "Way hay!" The kids fell about; and it was then that I knew I was in the same room as a comic genius. He was truly a legend. And do you know what? Not one swear word ever passed his lips. How times have changed!'

Eric and Ernie returned to BBC Television Centre to record the fourth series of *The Morecambe and Wise Show* in 1970. The five fortnightly editions of the show were broadcast from 1 July until 26 August that year. The first four were broadcast on BBC Two and the fifth on BBC One, the latter broadcast being designed to show viewers some of the antics the boys were getting up to on BBC Two! The guests in this series included Kenny Ball and his Jazzmen, Eric Porter, Jan Daley, Trio Athenee, George A. Cooper, Kenneth McKellar, Jenny Lee-Wright, Rex Rashley, Nina, Fenella Fielding, Barbara Murray, Dusty Springfield, Sir Michael Redgrave, Dame Flora Robson, Sir Felix Aylmer, Robin Day, Alan Curtis, Paul Anka, Ann Hamilton and Janet Webb.

Morecambe and Wise were Michael Aspel's guests on *Ask Aspel* on 16 October 1970. The BBC One programme featured a group of younger viewers posing questions to the comedy double act.

The duo returned to television again later that year for their second Christmas special. The show featured appearances from Peter Cushing, William Franklyn, Nina, Eric Porter, Edward Woodward, Kenny Ball and his Jazzmen, Alan Curtis, Rex Rashley, Ann Hamilton and Janet Webb. Highlights included William Franklyn appearing in one of Ernie's plays – this time a send-up of *The Three Musketeers*.

The following year, 1971, saw a busy diary of live shows for Eric and Ernie. These included three dates at Coventry Theatre on Friday 26, Saturday 27 and Sunday 28 February. Performances took place each evening at 6.00pm and 8.30pm. The publicity material displayed both pre-decimal and decimal ticket prices, as the United Kingdom and Ireland had decimalised their currencies on 15 February 1971, known as 'Decimal Day'.

Morecambe and Wise posing for a publicity photograph taken during 1954
(Frank Bell/Shutterstock)

Eric and Ernie making one of their appearances on the television series
Val Parnell's Saturday Spectacular in 1960 (ITV/Shutterstock)

Morecambe and Wise relaxing with The Beatles while taking a break from taping a classic edition of *Two of a Kind* (*The Morecambe and Wise Show*) at ATV in December 1963 (*Daily Sketch*/Shutterstock)

Eric and Ernie discussing Sid and Dick's script for another edition of *Two of a Kind* (*The Morecambe and Wise Show*) with director, Colin Clews (ITV/Shutterstock)

Eric sports a fun wig during the making of a sketch for one of the duo's
ATV shows in the 1960s (ITV/Shutterstock)

A still of Morecambe and Wise in their first film for The Rank Organisation, *The Intelligence Men* (ITV/Shutterstock)

Eric and Ernie preparing to film a shot for *The Intelligence Men* at Pinewood Studios (ITV/Shutterstock)

The much-loved act, in the guise of traffic wardens Eric Simpson and
Ernest Clark, filming a scene on location at Waterloo Place in London
for their second, and arguably best, film for The Rank Organisation,
That Riviera Touch (ITV/Shutterstock)

The boys grab a kiss from Claudette (Suzanne Lloyd) in a scene from
That Riviera Touch (ITV/Shutterstock)

Morecambe and Wise as two travelling salesmen in a scene from
The Magnificent Two, the act's final film outing for The Rank Organisation
(Moviestore/Shutterstock)

Maggie Smith with Eric and Ernie backstage at The London Palladium in 1970 following that year's BAFTA awards ceremony, at which Morecambe and Wise were presented with the award for Best Entertainment Personality (Bob Dear/AP/Shutterstock)

Eric and Ernie pose for a publicity photo with Glenda Jackson on the set
of the famous 'Antony and Cleopatra' sketch in 1971
(Phillip Jackson/ANL/Shutterstock)

Morecambe and Wise appearing with Vanessa Redgrave in the play,
'Napoleon and Josephine'. The sketch was one of the many highlights in
The Morecambe and Wise Christmas Show in 1973 (Bill Cross/ANL/Shutterstock)

Eric attempts to upstage Ernie with one of his trusty pipes (ANL/Shutterstock)

The double act and Penelope Keith share a joke while preparing to record the play 'Cyrano de Bergerac' for *Eric and Ernie's Christmas* in 1977 (Monty Fresco/ANL/Shutterstock)

Morecambe and Wise, together with their wives, Joan and Doreen, entertain photographs at Heathrow Airport (ANL/Shutterstock)

A publicity photo of Eric and Ernie taken outside Thames Television's headquarters in Teddington (ANL/Shutterstock)

Morecambe and Wise cook up some mischief with Alec Guinness during a break from making *The Morecambe and Wise Christmas Special* in 1980 (Mike Hollist/ANL/Shutterstock)

On 8 April 1971, the fifth series of *The Morecambe and Wise Show*, consisting of seven editions, began on BBC Two. The guests in this series included Dame Flora Robson, Arthur Lowe (and other main cast members from the sitcom *Dad's Army*), Susan Maughan, Kenny Ball and his Jazzmen, Frank Ifield, Richard Caldicot, Grazina Frame, Jack Jones, Sheila Southern, Glenda Jackson, Mary Hopkin, Ronnie Hilton, Ian Carmichael, Matt Monro, Kiki Dee, Ann Hamilton and Janet Webb.

There were a great many highlights in this series. Arthur Lowe's appearance with other *Dad's Army* cast members in a send-up of the film *Mutiny on the Bounty* called *Monty on the Bonty* was particularly memorable. There was also Ernie meeting a fellow writer (played by Michael Ward) in a flat sketch. A slightly rewritten version of this sketch would find its way into one of Morecambe and Wise's shows made by Thames Television. In the latter version, Hugh Paddick, most well known for being one of the cast members of the BBC radio series *Round the Horne*, took on Ward's role. Arguably the best sketch of the series featured Glenda Jackson, making her first appearance with Morecambe and Wise, as Cleopatra in a wonderful parody of the classic Shakespeare play *Antony and Cleopatra*.

Series six of *The Morecambe and Wise Show* began a run of six editions on 19 September 1971. Other than the final edition, they were shown weekly. The other change saw the series broadcast in full on BBC One. The line-up of guests included Francis Matthews, Anita Harris, Cilla Black, Ronnie Carroll, Percy Thrower, John Mills, Mrs Mills, Nina, and Ann Hamilton. A classic sketch in which Cilla Black explained that her record company want to sign Ernie for a record deal is still one of the most repeated of the series. John Mills joining Eric and Ernie in Ernie's version of *Escape from Stalag 54* (written with the help of Eddie Braben, of course) was also a high point, although the duo acting as Tom Jones's new backing singers and dancers while he performs the song 'Exactly Like You' is probably still remembered as one of the most outstanding highlights of series six. Both of Eric's children have vivid memories of their father explaining his idea for the sketch while they were on holiday in their villa in Portugal.

Due to the success of Eric and Ernie's live dates in the first part of the year, *The Stage* newspaper announced Billy Marsh's plans for an autumn tour in the latter part of 1971:

Morecambe and Wise – Autumn Tour

Eric Morecambe and Ernie Wise, whose short tour earlier this year was a sell-out success in advance, are to carry out similar engagements in the autumn.

Billy Marsh of London Management, who have arranged the new tour, told *The Stage*, 'Eric and Ernie have suggested that the tour dates should be as widespread as possible, covering theatres and theatre-clubs as well as cinemas. I am delighted to have been able to arrange a suitable itinerary, which I am sure will result in outstanding business at the box office.'

The full tour, which will consist of twice-nightly performances at each venue, starts at Sheffield's Fiesta Club on September 17/18 and continues with shows at Exeter, Nottingham, Southampton, Peterborough, Birmingham and Ipswich, concluding at the Bristol Hippodrome on November 26/27.

Ray Alan and Lord Charles, Mrs Mills and Sheila Southern appear with Morecambe and Wise in all dates from Exeter (October 15/16) onwards and an all-star supporting company is currently being negotiated for the Fiesta Club, Sheffield.

Musical accompaniment for the entire tour will be provided by Johnny Wiltshire and his band.

The tour started the same week that marked the thirtieth anniversary since Eric and Ernie had first performed together in public as a double act.

7

The Golden Years

MORECAMBE AND WISE HAD now got into their stride with the television shows for the BBC. Already a host of classic moments had found their way into the can. But their 1971 Christmas special, broadcast at 8.00pm on Christmas Day, eclipsed everything that had gone before. The guests that year were Shirley Bassey, Glenda Jackson, André Previn, Frank Bough, Robert Dougall, Cliff Michelmore, Patrick Moore, Michael Parkinson, Eddie Waring, Los Zafiros, Dick Emery, Francis Matthews and Ann Hamilton.

Without doubt, the most remembered part of this special is the 'Grieg Piano Concerto' sketch. Although most people, including those who weren't even born at the time, will recall André Previn's appearance in this now legendary sketch, they might not realise that two other versions of it were made – without Previn. During the 1960s, Eric and Ernie performed the first version, written by Hills and Green, as part of one of their ATV shows. It's true that the pay-off doesn't have quite the same impact as the Previn version, but the sketch still raises laughter. Here's a brief extract of the dialogue:

Ernie:	What would you say to the London Symphony Orchestra if you met them?
Eric:	Hello boys, have you seen my sister?
Ernie:	Why would you say that?
Eric:	Well the last time I saw her she was with them.

The second version of the sketch was a recording for Eric and Ernie's 1964 LP, *Mr Morecambe Meets Mr Wise*. However, Eric was proudest of the third version of the 'Grieg Piano Concerto' sketch, which, of course, featured André Previn. 'Whatever we do in the rest of our careers, at best we can only equal that,' Morecambe admitted to his son, Gary, on Boxing Day 1971.

'The journey between Previn agreeing and Previn appearing in a piece of comedy brilliance was scary for my father,' explained Gary. 'His agent agreed to three rehearsal days, but then his mother fell ill over in the States, meaning he could only arrive the evening before the show recorded. Previn turned up at the studios claiming that he had learnt the script in the back of the taxi from the airport. There's a moment in the show where you can see my father relax, because he knows it's going to work.' The exchange went as follows:

André:	I'll get my baton.
Ernie:	Please do.
André:	It's in Chicago.
Eric:	'It's in Chicago!' Ha ha. Pow! I like him!

Tony Hare worked as the floor assistant on the sketch. 'The recording in front of the studio audience was the first time the orchestra saw Eric, Ernie and André performing it, hence lots of laughter from the musicians,' he recalls. 'I was wearing "cans" [earphones] and such was the hysteria in the control gallery, director John Ammonds could hardly call the camera shots through laughing. I remember Eric saying to Ammonds afterwards, "You won't edit any of it, will you?" John replied, "It will go out exactly as you did it." I'll never forget the look of sheer horror on André's face when Eric started playing the piano. He was brilliant – and a nice man as well.'

Comedian Eddie Izzard is an ardent admirer of the 'Grieg Piano Concerto' sketch. 'Eric did what no other performer had done, or I think could ever do to a guest,' he explained, 'and that was to pick André Previn up by the lapels of his jacket with such excellent mock violence and take him down a peg with fantastically silly logic – "I am playing all the right notes, but not necessarily in the right order." It's a brilliant sketch, highbrow and lowbrow at the same time, and for me is the perfect example of a piece that sums up Morecambe and Wise. Eric's timing, and impressively that of André Previn, is excellent.'

Izzard has a theory as to why people will still be watching Morecambe and Wise in years to come. 'Their comedy is based in character play, and is therefore timeless,' he said. 'This is because human character has never changed since the beginning of civilisation, and I don't think it ever will. Eric and Ernie would have been funny even back in Greek or Roman times.'

After the recording of the sketch, Johnny Ammonds spoke to André Previn about his skills as a comedy performer. 'I said, "You know André, with your comic timing, you could have been a very good comedian,"' recounted Johnny. 'He said, "John, I think I'm happier with the baton if you don't mind."'

During the seventies, Eric and Ernie made a commercial recording of the song 'We Get Along So Easily (Don't You Agree)'. During the song, Morecambe can be heard making a reference to the now-classic sketch. After asking Ern who the conductor is, he is relieved to discover that it isn't 'Andrew Preview', because he 'ruined' his version of the Grieg Piano Concerto!

Shirley Bassey also made a strong impact in that year's Christmas special. In an unforgettable sketch, Bassey performed the song 'Smoke Gets in Your Eyes' while the boys, who were playing scenery men, sabotaged her number. After various indignities, including getting her stiletto wedged in a polystyrene step, poor Shirley ends up walking off the set wearing one of Eric's hobnail boots. Shirley also sang 'Diamonds Are Forever' during the same show – but this time she was alone! To break the ice during rehearsals for her number, Eric walked up to Shirley, and eyeing her beautiful glittering dress, said to her, 'You look like a Brillo pad!'

In addition to their Christmas television special, Christmas Day 1971 saw BBC Radio 2 broadcast *Morecambe and Wise Sing Flanagan and Allen* – Eric and Ernie's 1971 LP of the same name. This record saw them perform a selection of songs made famous by fellow double act, Bud Flanagan and Chesney Allen.

Although singing 'Bring Me Sunshine' had become a popular way to end their shows, Eric and Ernie felt they needed another song for their repertoire. Friends of the double act, Tony Hatch and Jackie Trent, were asked to take on the challenge of penning a song. 'I wrote the song "Positive Thinking" specifically for Morecambe and Wise (my former wife, Jackie, co-wrote the lyrics),' said Tony. 'Eric and Ernie personally asked for something bright and cheerful that could work as an alternative television-show closer to their usual "Bring Me Sunshine". They also included "Positive Thinking" in their stage shows.

'"Positive Thinking" was my idea for the title. There had been a best-selling book in 1952 called *The Power of Positive Thinking* written by the so-called "father of positive thinking", Norman Vincent Peale. Even in the 1970s the phrase was still in regular use.

'I did a quick demo, and Eric and Ernie liked it immediately. A songwriter can't ask for more. Their huge viewing figures made the song instantly popular and they adopted it as their own. They also adapted it because, in fact, the melody they sing isn't quite "the tune what I wrote". Who cares? They made it famous, and the words "positive thinking" are now identified more with Morecambe and Wise than with Norman Vincent Peale!

'There is a coda to this story. One day, I was eating in Biagi's Restaurant in Upper Berkeley Street in London. Eric, with two or three others, was halfway through his meal at a nearby table. By then he and Ernie were regularly performing "Positive Thinking". Shortly after we received the menu, Eric crawled on all fours over to our table and shouted in my ear, "Here's some positive thinking – don't have the fish!" He then crawled back again to his own table. Being a small restaurant, nobody could miss seeing or hearing him. Only Eric

Morecambe could do that and not be asked to leave on account of disorderly conduct.'

In addition to 'Bring Me Sunshine' and 'Positive Thinking', Morecambe and Wise would sometimes perform 'Following You Around', 'Just Around the Corner' and 'We Get Along (Don't You Agree)' at the end of their shows.

The start of 1972 saw Eric and Ernie attend the unveiling of their wax effigies at Madame Tussauds in London, on Friday 11 February. Eric joked that his wax effigy resembled the then popular television presenter, Cliff Michelmore.

Morecambe and Wise were Michael Parkinson's guests on an edition of *Parkinson* first aired by BBC One on 11 November 1972. Also appearing on the programme was the actress Raquel Welch. Writer, comedian and Morecambe and Wise admirer, Simon Pegg, was spellbound by the programme when he saw it repeated by the BBC many years later. 'Eric's appearance confirmed that he was just as funny in real life,' said Pegg. 'He had funny bones and was funny to his very soul. I remember he told a story about how he had a heart attack so hilariously. It's extremely poignant to see it now.

'I met Ernie at the BAFTAs and I said to him how much Morecambe and Wise had inspired me. It probably didn't mean much to him, but I loved having the opportunity to tell him; they are legends.'

There were no editions of *The Morecambe and Wise Show* in 1972. Such was the success of their Christmas special in 1971, Eric and Ernie decided to concentrate on preparing for that year's Christmas show. It was also felt that the reduced schedule would benefit Eric's health. Another deciding factor was that the pressure of delivering the best scripts possible had resulted in writer Eddie Braben suffering a nervous breakdown; the task of writing the 1972 Christmas show was given to Barry Cryer and John Junkin. The guests taking part included Bruce Forsyth, Glenda Jackson, Jack Jones, Vera Lynn, Pete Murray, and Kenny Ball and his Jazzmen.

There were also cameos from several high-profile guests who had appeared in the double act's previous BBC shows. They took part in a running gag in which they revealed what had supposedly happened to them in their professional lives since working with Eric and Ernie. We discovered that Ian Carmichael had become a newsvendor, Fenella Fielding a railway guard, Eric Porter a binman, André Previn a bus conductor and Dame Flora Robson a tea lady at BBC Television Centre. Janet Webb, however, was shown to have come up in the world and be living in a stately home with a big car!

With no new television shows in 1972 for viewers to feast on, the Christmas special was eagerly awaited. The usual opening spot featured Eric playing practical jokes on poor Little Ern. A buzzer secreted in Morecambe's hand gave Wise an unexpected shock, before a flower squirted water in his face and a telescope left a black mark around his eye. Not to be outdone, Ernie presented his old pal with a present that squirted foam in his face. Later in the show, Vera Lynn (referred to by Eric as Gracie Fields) sang 'Pass Me By', with Morecambe and Wise as backing singers. Little Ern surpassed himself by writing two plays for this special: Glenda Jackson appeared in *Victoria and Albert* and Pete Murray in *Dawn Patrol*. The latter included scenes filmed on location at Sibson airfield, near Peterborough, which were directed by Ed Stuart. Bruce Forsyth's cameo appearance was made at the end of a sketch that featured Eric and Ernie as reindeers. Although, as previously mentioned, Barry Cryer and John Junkin wrote this Christmas special, the reindeer sketch was written by Mike Craig and Lawrie Kinsley.

Series seven of *The Morecambe and Wise Show* began on 7 January 1973. The weekly twelve-edition series was the longest Eric and Ernie ever made for the BBC. The guests included Cliff Richard, Vicki Carr, Robert Morley, Lulu, Rostal and Schaefer, Percy Edwards, Allan Cuthbertson, Damaris Hayman, Les Rawlings, Johnny Shannon, Henry Cooper, Susan Hampshire, Georgie Fame and Alan Price, Jenny Lee-Wright, Frank Finlay, Frank Williams, Grazina Frame, Anita Harris, Anthony Sharp, Hannah Gordon, Roy Castle, Pete Murray, Nana Mouskouri, Sooty with

Harry Corbett, Johnny Vyvyan, Peter Cushing, Bernie Winters, Wilma Reading, Ann Hamilton and Janet Webb. Series highlights included Cliff Richard appearing in the musical routine 'The Fleet's in Town'; a send-up of *The Sooty Show*, with Harry Corbett and Sooty joining Eric and Ernie at the end; and Peter Cushing attempting to get paid again before performing the song 'A Couple of Swells' with the double act.

During the making of series seven, the BBC's long-running arts series *Omnibus* made a film called *Morecambe and Wise: Fools Rush in*. The fly-on-the-wall style documentary gave an account of the rehearsal and recording of an edition of the show that featured Anita Harris and Anthony Sharp as guests. Interviews with Eric and Ernie, Eddie Braben and Johnny Ammonds were intercut with the behind-the-scenes footage. BBC One subsequently broadcast the programme for the first time on 18 February 1973; it was also repeated by the BBC as part of their *Programmes for Schools and Colleges* strand.

On 21 February 1973, Morecambe and Wise appeared on the first edition of *Val Meets the VIPs*. The programme was described by the BBC as follows: 'Valerie Singleton talks to people who have earned the title Very Important Persons. An audience of children will join in and put their questions to the VIPs who this week are Morecambe and Wise.'

1973 also saw Dennis Holman act as referee on the double act's new book, *Eric and Ernie – The Autobiography of Morecambe and Wise*. The book mainly consisted of an engaging interview with the duo, and gave readers a chance to learn about their story to date. In the same year, Eric was profiled by Kenneth Tynan in *Observer Magazine*.

On 28 October 1973, Eric and Ernie, with musical backing by the Johnny Wiltshire Orchestra, filmed their live stage act at Croydon's Fairfield Hall as a present for their manager, Billy Marsh. With jokes, routines, musical numbers and ad-libs, the film gives a true account of what audiences would have seen if they'd booked to see one of their 'bank raids' in the 1970s. Although the show was never meant to be shown on television, an edited version was first broadcast by Thames Television in 1987, and by Channel 5 in 2015.

Vanessa Redgrave, Hannah Gordon, John Hanson and the New Seekers were Eric and Ernie's guests on their Christmas special in 1973 – the first festive edition that Eddie Braben had written for Morecambe and Wise since 1971. Yehudi Menuhin, Rudolf Nureyev, Laurence Olivier and André Previn also appeared on film inserts showing them supposedly turning down the duo's invitations to appear on the show.

The special saw Eric informing Ernie he had been awarded the title 'Lord Ern of Peterborough' during the opening spot. Later, Hannah Gordon attempted to sing 'The Windmills of Your Mind' while competing with a large gust of wind generated by a windmill behind her. A bedroom sketch also brought laughter, not least from the following two lines:

Ern: You'll have sciatica in the morning.
Eric: I won't, I'll have Shredded Wheat like
        everybody else.

Vanessa Redgrave (renamed Vanilla Redgrave by Eric) taking on the role of Empress Josephine in Ernie's play *Napoleon and Josephine* was another highlight of that year's special. Redgrave also impressed viewers by taking part in a mambo dance routine with the boys.

Christmas at the Morecambe household would also include a viewing of that year's special. Even Eric would laugh loudly as he watched the programme. At the same time, the comedian was always keen to see the reactions of his family. He was only able to fully relax if he was satisfied with the show and his family's reactions.

Morecambe and Wise were both honoured by the Variety Club of Great Britain in May 1974. Performers and friends gathered at the Dorchester Hotel to pay tribute to the two men, who had first met thirty-five years before in 1939. The luncheon was introduced by Ray Moore and broadcast by the BBC on 14 May. The well-known personalities present included André

Previn, Glenda Jackson, Robert Morley, Robin Day, Graham Hill and Francis Matthews.

Two months later, Eric and Ernie were the first guests in a new series called *André Previn Meets...* Broadcast by BBC One on 14 July 1974, the programme was described by the BBC as: 'First of a series of informal conversations between the musical maestro and his friends and acquaintances in various walks of life.'

In a big step for Eric and Joan, the couple adopted a boy, called Steven, in 1974. Steven had come into their lives when Eric's daughter, Gail, had been working at the adoption home where he had been living. Gail used to take Steven to Eric and Joan's home in Harpenden as a treat. The adoption home later approached Eric and Joan and asked if they would like to foster Steven. They weren't keen because of Eric's high profile, but the suggestion that they officially adopt Steven was agreed following a family meeting.

Life for Eric's children was always going to be unique. His daughter, Gail, once shared her views on their home life. 'He was funny. If nothing was happening, a pair of glasses would suddenly appear around the door. My brother, Gary, summed it up perfectly when he said, "It's like living in the twilight zone of a situation comedy."' For example, on one occasion, Eric walked into the house, having just returned home from BBC Television Centre and a visit to the studio hairdresser.

Cue the following exchange:

Gary: Hi, Dad. I like the haircut.
Eric: Good.
Gary: It makes you look like Sean Connery.
Eric: Yes. A very Shorn Connery.

Series eight of *The Morecambe and Wise Show* began on 27 September 1974. Following the completion of this series, Johnny Ammonds would not work with Eric and Ernie again until they moved to Thames Television. The guests in the six editions included André Previn, Magnus Magnusson, Wilma Reading, Mrs Mills, Ludovic Kennedy, Allan Cuthbertson, the Syd Lawrence Orchestra, Grazina Frame, Richard Baker, Frank Finlay, Susan Hampshire, Glenda Jackson, Francis Matthews, Hughie Green, David Dimbleby, June Whitfield, John Quayle, Jenny Lee-Wright, Ann Hamilton and Arthur Tolcher. Amongst the highlights in this series were a send-up of *Mastermind* featuring the then host Magnus Magnusson, and June Whitfield appearing in Ernie's play *The Plantation of Passion*.

It's no secret that Morecambe and Wise were huge admirers of Laurel and Hardy. By their own admission, their earliest comedy routines were heavily influenced by their heroes, having seen practically every film the double act ever made. Eric and Ernie even booked to see Stan and Ollie performing live on stage at the Embassy

Theatre, Peterborough. The chance to meet did present itself when the boys were in pantomime at the Lyceum Theatre and Laurel and Hardy were appearing in their show at the Empire Theatre. Unfortunately, they missed them and the opportunity for the two acts to meet never presented itself again. Appropriately, Morecambe and Wise were asked to narrate a Laurel and Hardy documentary called *Cuckoo – A Celebration of Stan Laurel and Oliver Hardy*. First broadcast by the BBC in December 1974, the film was shown as part of the long-running *Omnibus* series.

There was no new Christmas special on television in 1974. Instead, Michael Parkinson interviewed Eric and Ernie in a programme that also featured clips from their previous shows. Mike Yarwood was given the usual spot reserved for *The Morecambe and Wise Christmas Show*, and *Parkinson Takes a Christmas Look at Morecambe and Wise* was broadcast straight afterwards.

January 1975 saw Eric and Ernie return to BBC radio with the start of a series of seven programmes on BBC Radio 2 called *The Eric Morecambe and Ernie Wise Show*. (The seventh edition of the series was held over until July and broadcast as a 'summer special'.) Written by Eddie Braben, who mainly adapted the material he had written for Eric and Ernie's television programmes, and produced by John Browell, the series was recorded at the BBC's Paris Studio on Lower Regent Street in

London; guests taking part in the first series included Michael Segal, Peters and Lee, Salena Jones, Michael Ward, Anita Harris, Wilma Reading, Laura Lee, Lynsey de Paul, Ann Hamilton and Arthur Tolcher.

The Paris Studio had an interesting history. Located underground, it was originally built as a cinema called, not surprisingly given its later name, the Paris Cinema. Its days as a picture house, however, were short-lived. It opened on 20 April 1939 with Jean Renoir's film *La Bête Humaine*. The following year saw the government Office of Works requisition the building. Eventually the BBC took it over and turned it into a studio. Many classic radio shows that required studio audiences, including *Round the Horne*, *Dad's Army* and *The News Huddlines*, were recorded there. In addition to comedy shows, the studio also played host to concert performances by AC/DC, The Beatles, David Bowie, Family, Jeff Beck, Deep Purple, Dr Feelgood, Fleetwood Mac, Genesis, Led Zeppelin, Joni Mitchell, Pink Floyd, Rod Stewart and Simple Minds. During John Birt's tenure at the BBC, the corporation decided not to renew their lease and moved out in early 1995. The studio has since been turned into a gym, and a swimming pool now takes the place of the rows of seating.

On 31 March 1975, *Eric and Ernie's Hall of Fame* was broadcast by BBC Radio 4. A second part, entitled *Eric and Ernie's Second Hall of Fame*, hit the airwaves on Christmas Day. Meanwhile, Morecambe and Wise's 'bank-raid' appearances that year included a string of Sunday shows at the Britannia Pier Theatre in Great Yarmouth, not far from the Wellington Pier where the double act had appeared in their successful summer season in 1964.

Eric gave his daughter, Gail, away at her wedding to her first husband, Paul Jarvis, at St Nicholas Church, Harpenden, on 6 September 1975. Ernie and his wife, Doreen, were guests, and a photo was taken of Eric and Ernie kissing the bride on each cheek. As footage filmed at the wedding reception proves, Eric's speech brought much hilarity to the proceedings.

8

Bank Raids and High Ratings

BILL COTTON CALLED ERNEST Maxin into his office one day and told him that Eric and Ernie wanted him to take over as producer and director on their show. Ernest initially had misgivings. He and Johnny Ammonds were good friends (in fact, their offices were located right next door to each other at BBC Television Centre) and so Ernest's concern was understandable. However, it was Johnny's decision to leave the show. He was keen for a change and wanted to work on the 1976 series of *Look, Mike Yarwood!* Also, Johnny's wife was ill, and understandably he wanted to spend more time with her at home.

Ernest Maxin (who, as previously mentioned, had first worked with Morecambe and Wise on *Running Wild*) had already helped Johnny with ideas for routines for *The Morecambe and Wise Show*. For instance, he had created the famous hobnail boot routine for Shirley Bassey for the Christmas special back in 1971, and had also worked on routines featuring Glenda Jackson and Vanessa Redgrave. He had an enviable track record in producing and directing light entertainment for television and, like Eric and Ernie, he was also Hollywood-mad; so it was a professional marriage made in heaven. With everyone's blessing, Ernest was given the job of producing and directing all future editions of *The Morecambe and Wise Show* for the BBC.

There was no television series of the show in 1975. To placate the viewers, however, there was a Christmas special. This show saw Ernest Maxin taking over the reins officially for the first time. The guests included Diana Rigg, Des O'Connor, Gordon Jackson, Robin Day, Diane Solomon, Brenda Arnau, Pan's People, Reg Turner, Debbie Ash, Fiona Grey and Ann Hamilton.

One of the classic sketches of Morecambe and Wise's BBC era featured the guest appearance of Des O'Connor. Des had long been the butt of many of Eric and Ernie's jokes. Now he had finally been given a chance to come face to face with the duo and to get his own back. It must be remembered that the three men were real-life friends. Des (which Eric claimed was 'short for desperate') has always been quick to point out that he had a hand in some of the jokes. 'Quite a lot of his insults I wrote myself,' Des once explained. 'Things like, "Des O'Connor's a self-made man. Well, it's nice of him to take the blame."' Although a prop Des O'Connor record without a hole in the middle survives in Eric Morecambe's family archive, Eric was in reality a fan of O'Connor's music. His wife, Joan, once told Des that she went into Eric's study one day to find him listening to one of his records!

Eddie Braben's opening spot in the 1975 Christmas special featuring O'Connor with Morecambe and Wise included many funny lines. Exactly how many were ad-libbed by the three performers is hard to say. Arguably, the best line in the sketch was delivered by Eric, who declared, 'God, if you want me to be a goner, get me an LP by Des O'Connor.'

Other highlights in the special included Diana Rigg playing the title role in a rip-roaring parody of *Nell Gwynne*. This ended with a song-and-dance routine to 'How Could You Believe Me When I Said I Love You When You Know I've Been a Liar All My Life?' Gordon Jackson, who played butler Angus Hudson in the popular LWT drama series *Upstairs, Downstairs*, also made a cameo appearance in the sketch. Another classic moment featured Eric and Ernie, dressed as female dancers, performing a dance routine with Pan's People while Brenda Arnau sang 'Big Spender'.

The start of 1976 saw the untimely death of Eric's father, George Bartholomew, on 2 January. He was buried in Torrisholme Cemetery, Morecambe. His death marked the end of his marriage to Sadie, which had lasted almost fifty years.

The final series of *The Morecambe and Wise Show* made by the BBC began on 7 January 1976. Ernest Maxin produced and directed the six editions and Eddie Braben wrote the scripts. The guests who appeared in this, their ninth series, included Peter O'Sullivan, Gilbert O'Sullivan, Dilys Watling, the Vernons, Michele Dotrice, Frankie Vaughan, Tammy Jones, Patrick Moore, Lena Zavaroni, the Spinners, Allan Cuthbertson, Jackie Darnell, Anthony Sharp, Diane Solomon, Champagne, Maggie Fitzgibbon, Ann Hamilton and Arthur Tolcher. Some of the biggest highlights of the series were the song-and-dance numbers. Michele Dotrice performed 'Nobody Does it Like Me' and Lena Zavaroni sang 'Something 'Bout Ya Baby I Like'. There was also a unique take on 'Slaughter on Western Avenue'.

Michele Dotrice felt honoured to be asked to appear with Eric and Ernie. 'It was at the time, and still would be to this day, the most incredible accolade to be asked to guest in a play wot Ernie wrote,' she said. 'They were the gentlest of gentlemen in the business, but it was an absolute impossibility not to laugh when working with them! If they knew you were prone to the giggles, like what I am, you'd had it! They were the most supreme artistes, who honed every sketch within an inch of its life, searching ever more for another laugh. I miss them so much.'

Edition four of series nine, first broadcast on 10 March 1976, featured an often-repeated tap-dancing sketch which saw a troupe of top-hat-and-tailed male dancers doing their very best to block Eric and Ernie from the viewers' gaze. One of the dancers was David Schulten. 'I ended up rolling around on the floor with Eric at the end of the routine. I was appearing in the musical *Billy* with Eric's great pal Roy Castle at the time. Eric came to see the show on his fiftieth birthday. After the show ended, there was a knock on the dressing-room door and a pair of glasses appeared around the door before Eric walked in. You must remember, I was just a chorus boy, and yet Eric had taken the trouble to look up my name, walk up six floors to find me and tell me he had enjoyed the show. He also said he hoped we'd work together again one day. I say this to demonstrate the measure of the man. I subsequently worked with Morecambe and Wise again at Thames and asked for

Eric's autograph – something I rarely did, but I felt impelled to on this occasion. Eric signed: "To David, it's always a pleasure to work with you. Best wishes, Eric Morecambe, 1882"! This was in 1982 and, as he handed it to me, he said, "There you are sunshine, it's an antique already." They were two of the greats. Eric wouldn't have touched the heights that he did without Ernie. Eric truly was a master comic and a decent man.'

The breakfast scene featuring Eric and Ernie dancing around their fictious kitchen to David Rose's song 'The Stripper' remains one of the duo's most iconic and repeated sketches. Yet it was only devised when Ernest Maxin realised that the sixth edition of series nine was going to underrun. There wasn't time for a new sketch to be written and learnt, and there was already a dance number in the show. Maxin assured Eric and Ernie he had an idea in his head for a sketch that would be visual. What's more, he would rehearse the routine with them the following day.

The truth was that he didn't have any idea at that stage. Thankfully, listening to the radio in the car on the way home from rehearsals gave Ernest the inspiration he needed to devise the sketch. 'I heard the music for "The Stripper" and I thought, there's something here, but I couldn't think how to do it. And you know, the harder you try to think, the more solid concrete sets between the ears.

'When I got home, my wife, Leigh, said, "What's the matter with you?" I must have looked drawn and worried. I explained what had happened. She said, "Don't worry about that. Why don't you go to bed early? Get a good night's sleep and I'll have breakfast ready for you. What do you want? Do you want grapefruit? Toast?" I said, "Wait a minute." I wrote that down and suddenly I could see something, but I didn't know what.

'I went into the kitchen singing this tune and opening and closing the cupboards. Suddenly it all came to me, so I wrote the top line down on a piece of paper. I did the mixing of the omelettes, now with all those things and the toast popping up, the chopping of the grapefruit, to plant that. 'The music has got to be written to fit the gag, not just play the song through. When Ernie was mixing the omelette, I needed the brass to flare. Silence when he took a breather. The chopping of the grapefruit, then separating them, squeezing them. I rang Peter Knight (who was the musical arranger and conductor on the series) and went through what I wanted note by note. He was terrific. You only had to tell Peter once. I knew I wouldn't have to worry and that it would be there at nine o'clock the following morning.' The idea meeting with the double act's approval, the sketch was duly taped and included in that week's show.

Although Ernest Maxin was held in high esteem by Eric and Ernie, this would not stop him from becoming the victim of practical jokes set up by the double act. Arriving home one day from location filming for *The Morecambe and Wise Show*, Maxin discovered that he had a black ink ring around one of his eyes after the duo had added black ink to the eye piece on the camera. In fact, he recalled getting some very strange looks while he was travelling home on a tube train in London!

It's Childsplay, a series in which Morecambe and Wise introduced short plays written entirely by young playwrights under sixteen, whom they met during each of the programmes, began its six-week run on BBC One on 30 July 1976. Guest stars included Alfie Bass, Ralph Bates, Rudolph Walker, Arthur Lowe, Sinead Cusack, Ian Ogilvy, Michael Aldridge, Blake Butler, Peter Jones, Penelope Keith, Peter Sallis, Zena Walker, Christopher Cazenove, Glynn Edwards, Carmel McSharry, Angharad Rees, Keith Barron and Dora Bryan.

The second series of *The Eric Morecambe and Ernie Wise Show* began on BBC Radio 2 on 5 September 1976. As with the previous series, the six new thirty-minute editions were written by Eddie Braben and mostly based on the scripts he'd written for the television shows. The guests taking part in the shows included Gayle Hunnicutt, Richard Caldicot, April Walker, Percy Edwards, Salena Jones, Clodagh Rodgers, Nicola

Pagett, Elaine Delmar, Brian Wilde and Ann Hamilton. Tom Edwards was the announcer on five of the six editions of the 1976 radio series. 'Eric and Ernie were fun and most generous to me as the announcer, and we got on well,' said Tom. 'They also involved me in one of the plays wot Ernie wrote! I was speaking to Nicola Pagett, one of the guests on the show, one day in the green room. We were talking about the theatre and I accidentally mentioned the name of "the Scottish play" by William Shakespeare. Nicola went white and told me off because it's bad luck to mention the title. In the event, all was well. But I never forgot that!'

There were further live appearances by Morecambe and Wise in 1976. These 'bank raids' included their very last-ever stage performance in Blackpool, which took place at the Opera House on 23 October 1976.

In November that year, Eric and Ernie visited Buckingham Palace to receive their OBEs from the Queen. Outside the Palace, they posed for the cameras with Welsh rugby star Mervyn Davies. Newsreel footage filmed after the ceremony showed that Eric's wife, Joan, and Ernie's wife, Doreen, were in attendance, along with Eric's children, Gail and Gary, and Ernie's mother, Connie. Eric joked to journalists that they had each been given OBEs so they wouldn't have to take turns wearing the same one. Both men were also honoured with the Freedom of the City of London in 1976.

Comedian Jim Davidson first met Eric Morecambe when he was appearing in panto at the Alexandra Theatre in Birmingham during Christmas 1976. 'We did a midnight matinee and, although it wasn't particularly a dirty version, it did send the panto up,' said Jim. 'Eric appeared in the show and I remember that at one point he stuck his glasses in front of the curtains and brought the house down!'

Eric and Ernie's Christmas special in 1976 was called simply *The Morecambe and Wise Show*; for some reason the word 'Christmas' didn't appear in the title. The programme was written by Barry Cryer and John Junkin due to the unavailability of Eddie Braben. Mike Craig, Lawrie Kinsley and Ron McDonnell also contributed material. The show remains a classic, with guests including Elton John, John Thaw, Dennis Waterman, Kate O'Mara, Marion Montgomery and The Nolan Sisters taking part. But the biggest talking point that year was the appearance of Angela Rippon – and her legs!

The journey to get Angela onto the show was a long and complicated one for Ernest Maxin, as he explained during an interview many years later. It was a quest that began when Angela visited the studio at BBC Television Centre where Eric and Ernie were preparing for their next show. 'We'd broken for lunch,' said Maxin. 'Down the iron staircase into the studio came Angela Rippon with an aunt of hers from Devon. The aunt wanted to look around Morecambe and Wise's studio and I said yes, she could.

'It was the first time I'd seen Angela from the waist down. Now, I saw these gorgeous legs and said, "Do you dance at all?" She replied, "Well, I went to a dancing school, and I love ballet." I asked if she'd like to come on to *The Morecambe and Wise Show*, and she said, "I'd love to, but I don't think my boss would let me." I said, "Would you mind if I went to see him?" So I did, and he said he didn't mind, providing that if it didn't work, I wouldn't use it. I replied, "For my sake, I wouldn't."

'The next week at rehearsals, I told Eric and Ernie the story, adding, "I think it would be a great news thing, because the public have only ever seen her from the waist up sitting behind a desk." Ernie thought it was a great idea, but Eric said no. I would never make him do anything, but it was playing on my mind.

'A couple of shows later, Eric came to me and said they'd been invited to the Lady Taverners' lunch at Lords. He was a keen cricket fan. Sometimes, in the middle of rehearsals when things were getting a bit overpowering, we'd stop and chalk a wicket on the wall, and I had a tennis ball and a bat there, so we could play for a bit. Anyway, I knew about this invitation before he said it – I won't tell you how – but I also knew Angela was going to be there. I said, "Okay, but you'll have to work later in the evening."

'What happened was, my staff knew Angela was going to be there, and I had my production manager and my secretary there; and when the boys came back to rehearsals I was expecting them to say, "Okay, let's have Angela in the show" – but nothing was said. We just carried on rehearsing, and at the end I thought, it's all over now, we tried. They leant over, said goodnight and Eric was the last one to go. He closed the door as he went out; a few seconds later, he put his head around the door, and, smoking his pipe, said, "Let's have Angela Rippon in the show." The idea worked and became a talking point.'

Angela's high-kicking routine began with the newsreader behind a desk pretending to read a newsflash. On cue, the desk split in two to reveal that she was wearing a fetching outfit that showed off her legs. She then launched into a song-and-dance routine with Eric and Ernie that featured the songs 'Let's Face the Music and Dance' and 'A – You're Adorable'. Without doubt, it was one of the biggest highlights of that year's Christmas show.

In 2011, the production team on *Strictly Come Dancing* invited Angela to recreate the routine for that year's *Children in Need* special joined by Sian Williams, Sophie Raworth, Susanna Reid and Emily Maitlis. The sequence began with the presenters sitting behind their desks wearing geeky glasses, white blouses and pencil skirts, before launching into a raunchy dance routine in glittery purple leotards.

One of the other highlights of the Christmas special in 1976 was the duo's version of *Singin' in the Rain*. Ernie took on the Gene Kelly role and sang and danced to the song while the heavens, well, didn't open. The studio and Ernie remained dry. The only one who got wet was Eric, who played the police officer. At one point in the sketch, Ernie throws his umbrella into the air and fails to catch it before it falls onto the floor. This was deliberate and inspired by a moment in the rehearsal room when Ernest Maxin accidentally dropped the umbrella while showing Ernie the routine and everyone laughed. Patricia Ward Kelly, Gene's Kelly's widow, says her husband approved of the affectionate send-up of the iconic scene from the 1952 Hollywood musical. 'Gene was a fan of British comedians, including Morecambe and Wise,' she explained. 'When he was honoured by the Variety Club in London in May 1980, they screened the Morecambe and Wise version of *Singin' in the Rain* and Gene said it was "probably the most entertaining thing I've ever seen".'

Although 1977 proved to be an important year for Morecambe and Wise, the year also brought sadness as Eric's mother, Sadie, passed away on 7 May. She was buried with her husband in Morecambe.

In the run-up to their Christmas special in 1977, Eric and Ernie performed a host of live shows. Their schedule included appearing at the Alhambra Theatre,

Bradford, on Friday 3 and Saturday 4 June at 6.15pm and 9.00pm. Later that month they played Newcastle City Hall on Saturday 25 June at 9.00pm as part of the Newcastle Festival, which was sponsored by Alcan (UK) Ltd. They also performed on four Sundays (10 and 24 July and 7 and 21 August) at the Pavilion Theatre, Bournemouth. Performances took place at 6.10pm and 8.30pm on each of the dates.

Eric's son, Gary, helped to sell merchandise, including souvenir programmes and T-shirts, in the foyer of Morecambe and Wise's live shows in 1977. 'If sales were slow, I'd tell them my father was Eric Morecambe,' said Gary. 'But mostly they laughed and walked away. The truth is often tougher to sell than fiction.

'The funniest occasion was at the Floral Hall, Scarborough, when the box-office lady told me with a sigh that I was about the third person claiming to be his son that day. Then my Dad turned up at the box office and gave me a hug, and her jaw dropped!

'When I rewrote the souvenir brochure for that year's "bank raids", my father was thrilled. He said it added an authenticity that had been lacking in the previous version. It was my first published work!'

On 6 June 1977, BBC One broadcast a programme called *The Music of Morecambe and Wise*. The special featured Michael Parkinson talking to Eric and Ernie and introducing some of the musical highlights from the

BBC editions of *The Morecambe and Wise Show* from over the years. The clips included Vanessa Redgrave, Cliff Richard, Diana Rigg and Angela Rippon.

In July, Eric was presented by Princess Alexandra with an Honorary Degree from Lancaster University. 'Eric was immensely proud at receiving a doctorate,' said Eric's widow, Joan. 'He didn't expect that and that meant a lot to him. But his proudest moment was having his children.'

Eric and Ernie recorded the third series *of The Eric Morecambe and Ernie Wise Show*, which featured four editions including *The Eric Morecambe and Ernie Wise Christmas Show*, at the BBC Paris Studio during 1977. The series was originally broadcast weekly on BBC Radio 2 from the 4 to 25 December that same year. The guests included Allan Cuthbertson, Anita Harris, Des O'Connor, Marion Montgomery, Vince Hill and Ann Hamilton. Once again, Eddie Braben adapted his scripts for radio.

The year 1977 also saw Eric resign as a director of Luton Town FC and instead become their vice-president. This released the comedian from his boardroom and financial responsibilities.

On Christmas Eve 1977, Eric appeared on *World of Sport*. The weekly ITV series, which was based in Studio 5 at LWT's studios on the South Bank in London, was hosted by Morecambe's friend Dickie Davies. Davies invited the comedian to make a guest appearance on the programme, and attend their Christmas party, while having lunch at the Savoy Grill. Dickie had no idea what the comedian was going to say or do. To the delight of the viewers and the crew in the studio, Eric proceeded to deliver a host of funny lines and perform his paper bag trick while Dickie attempted to somehow keep the programme together.

Arguably the pinnacle of their television career, Morecambe and Wise's last-ever Christmas special for BBC television, entitled *Morecambe and Wise's Christmas Show*, was broadcast on Christmas Day in 1977. Eddie Braben was back on board as scriptwriter; meanwhile, Ernest Maxin produced and directed the show – his last for Eric and Ernie.

After Angela Rippon's appearance in the 1976 Christmas special was aired, both Richard Baker and Michael Aspel asked Ernest Maxin if they could appear with Morecambe and Wise in a future show. This gave Maxin the idea to create a routine for the 1977 special that was based around the *South Pacific* song 'There is Nothing Like a Dame'. In addition to Aspel and Baker, Frank Bough, Philip Jenkinson, Kenneth Kendall, Barry Norman, Michael Parkinson, Eddie Waring, Richard Whitmore and Peter Woods were all booked to appear with Eric and Ernie in the sketch. Due to their various schedules, it proved impossible for Maxin to bring all the presenters together in the rehearsal room at the same time. On the Wednesday, with the sketch due to be taped on the Saturday, Eric began to express his doubts about whether it would work. Ernest tried to assure him that it would work because all of them would be present at the recording. Unable to convince him, it was down to Ernie to reassure him. 'Look, if it doesn't work, we don't use it,' he said. If it hadn't been for Ernie, Maxin would have had to drop the number from the show.

The whole routine was rehearsed and taped the following Saturday in just thirty minutes. Ernie wasn't worried in the slightest, but Eric was still not convinced the routine was going to work. To alleviate his fears, Ernest invited Morecambe to come to the edit suite at eleven o'clock that evening, and he agreed to attend. 'I watched his face,' said Ernest. 'I could see the reflection in the screen. He was sitting back. As it went on, he began to lean forward; and when it came to the dance routine, where it all fitted, I saw there were tears running down his face. It moved me, it really moved me. He said, "Bloody hellfire, Ernest, it works." He put his arms around me and gave me a hug.'

The sketch was subsequently shown to the studio audience during the main recording the following evening. Thanks to the clever editing, some of the public thought the tricky acrobatics were really performed by the cast! 'Richard Baker came into my office,' recalled Maxin. 'He said, "I'm in trouble. I've been invited to open a fête and do my acrobatic trick. What can I do? I can't give the game away." I said, "Just tell them you're on duty that day."'

Other highlights in the Christmas special in 1977 included a parody of the opening title sequence to the action drama *Starsky and Hutch*, which they renamed *Starkers and Krutch*. Elton John (nicknamed Elephant and John by Eric) made several appearances as he desperately made his way around BBC Television Centre in attempt to find Eric and Ernie's studio. Along the way, he came face to face with John Laurie, John Le Mesurier and Arthur Lowe relaxing in a sauna while dressed in their *Dad's Army* costumes. The running gag ended with Elton performing for two female cleaners (Eric and Ernie dressed up) in an empty studio. Another running gag saw Angela Rippon dancing with a chorus line of dancers.

Penelope Keith also found her attempt to take part in one of Morecambe and Wise's famous song-and-dance routines was thwarted by an unfinished staircase. This led to the indignity of having to climb down onto the studio floor, while dressed to the nines, with the aid of Eric and Ernie.

The other guests appearing that year included Angharad Rees, Francis Matthews, Richard Briers, Paul

Eddington, James Hunt, Jenny Lee-Wright and Valerie Leon. It was estimated that over twenty-eight million viewers watched the show when it was broadcast on Christmas night. The schedule on BBC One that evening went as follows:

7.15pm	*Bruce Forsyth and The Generation Game*
8.20pm	*Mike Yarwood Christmas Special*
8.55pm	*Morecambe and Wise Christmas Special*
10.00pm	News
10.05pm	*Funny Girl*

Although they were riding high on the crest of the ratings, Morecambe and Wise were about to shock the BBC and the viewers in equal measure by announcing they were leaving the Corporation. Bill Cotton, who had signed Eric and Ernie to the BBC, was about to take over as Controller of BBC One. According to Cotton, Eric informed him at a party at BBC Television Centre that he and Ernie had received an offer to sign to Thames Television. Bill later claimed he offered to match the deal. As it was a social situation, and thus not appropriate to discuss business, no more was said. Bill must have believed a conversation with their agent, Billy Marsh, would have been on the cards for the start of 1978.

After Christmas, Bill travelled to America. He was sitting in a hotel one day, feeling low with a flu-type illness, when the phone rang. It was his secretary, who informed him of the news that Morecambe and Wise had signed to Thames. After such a long and successful association, Bill admitted that their departure felt like a 'divorce'.

Their new highly lucrative deal with the then ITV London weekday franchise-holder saw Eric and Ernie leave their old spiritual home of BBC Television Centre at White City and move to Thames' then headquarters in Teddington, Middlesex. They were to remain with the company for the rest of their careers together.

9

The Thames Years

T HE START OF 1978 saw Eric and Ernie appear as guests on Denis Norden's nostalgia-based show, *Looks Familiar*. Also guesting on the Thames Television programme on ITV was the actress Patricia Hayes. The duo later appeared together on another edition of the show the following April; this time, the other guest was the *Coronation Street* actress Betty Driver.

The beginning of 1978 also saw the recording of two final editions of *The Eric Morecambe and Ernie Wise Show* at the BBC Paris Studio on Lower Regent Street. They were all the programmes that would form series four of this popular radio series. They were broadcast

on BBC Radio 2 on 25 March and 1 May 1978. Eddie
Braben was once more brought in to adapt his own
television scripts; the guests included Penelope Keith,
Vincent Zara, Allan Cuthbertson, The Nolan Sisters
and Ann Hamilton. With their last two radio shows
recorded, this marked the end of all of Morecambe and
Wise's commitments for the BBC.

The reasons for their switch back to ITV, and who
instigated the move, are unclear. However, Ernie was
close friends with Philip Jones, who was then head of
light entertainment at Thames Television. The number
of hit series Jones green-lit during his career was
remarkable. During his time at Thames, Jones was
responsible for signing Benny Hill and Tommy Cooper
for the company, and for commissioning a raft of
sitcoms including *Father, Dear Father*, *Bless this House*,
Man About the House and *George and Mildred*. Even
after he 'retired', Philip continued to work, becoming
an executive producer on programmes made by Benny
Hill, and on most editions of the BBC television sitcom,
As Time Goes By. It would not be an exaggeration to say
that Jones pulled off a huge coup by tempting Eric and
Ernie away from the BBC. Although money may have
been an important factor, the chance to make a new
film was also partly the reason why the duo moved to
Thames. They had always wanted to do another comedy
film, and were keen to try something new.

Morecambe and Wise's first major project for Thames turned out to be for their offshoot company, Euston Films. Originally, Euston were known for making drama series on film for Thames, most famously *The Sweeney* and later *Minder*. John Thaw and Dennis Waterman had, of course, appeared on Eric and Ernie's Christmas special in 1976; this was at a time when they were both starring in *The Sweeney*. After John and Dennis's appearance on their show was recorded, Eric and Ernie said they wanted to appear in an episode of *The Sweeney*. Due to their BBC contract, this would have been out of the question at the time, but now they were signed to Thames, it was a real possibility.

Writer and producer Ted Childs couldn't believe their luck. 'We thought initially that it was a joke,' he said. 'But then, when we realised they were serious, we had to decide what kind of episode we could contrive for Eric and Ernie. We decided that, whatever we did, they should play themselves. Accordingly, the late Donald Churchill and I set out to write a script. We had to struggle somewhat to avoid the script falling between two stools, i.e. being neither comedy nor action drama. I must confess I have not seen the film for many years now, but I like to think we pulled it off. Of course, Eric and Ernie made their own very special contribution to the script, which was what we really all wanted.

'*The Sweeney* in those days was geared to be a very cost-effective production, and staying on schedule was a vital ingredient of our modus operandi. Although Eric and Ernie were very professional and fitted in with the "kick bollocks scramble" that characterised our production methods, their natural comedy and frequent ad-libs brought us all to near hysteria on occasions, with the whole cast and crew corpsed with fits of uncontrollable laughter. There were times when, as the man responsible, I wondered if we would ever complete the schedule. We did, of course. Eric and Ernie were aided and abetted by John and Dennis, both of whom were closet comics.

'Although we used stuntmen for the action stuff, we asked our actors to do as much energetic stuff as was consistent with their own safety and our insurance policy. Again, I recall that Eric and Ernie were very keen to play an active part.'

Mike Vardy, the director, has mixed memories of working on the episode, which was called 'Hearts and Minds'. 'I was asked to direct because none of my fellow directors had experience in comedy,' recalled Vardy. 'I had done work by the late great Jack Rosenthal, and Donald Churchill himself. Drama directors in the main felt they could confine themselves only to drama. I was proud to think I was asked to do the production, but maybe not so proud of the result; but then that is my self-critical self at work. I had trouble trying to mould the different styles together, and it is fair to say I think I failed.

'I was a great fan of theirs and therefore up for what I knew would be a challenge. They were consummate professionals and gave us all a lot of enjoyment and laughs, and because of that they won the respect of the whole cast and crew who were their usual disciplined selves. Eric and Ernie were who they were, and all they had to do was work inside their metier, which they knew so well. They never turned up without knowing every single line of dialogue, and during the scenes of possible physical danger would listen to the stunt arranger and follow his advice. I believe it did well with audiences when transmitted, which was the whole idea from the start.' It's worth noting that an assertion from Eric and Ernie reveals that they thought their work on *The Sweeney* was the best they had ever done on film.

As part of Morecambe and Wise's contract with Thames they were committed to taping new shows, including Christmas editions, for the company. These were broadcast on the ITV network. The pressure to come up with new ideas was still there; but at first their chief writer, Eddie Braben, was not. Although they did not make a full series in 1978, Eric and Ernie did make two specials. The first, called *The Morecambe and Wise Show*, was broadcast on 18 October, and also starred

Donald Sinden, Judi Dench, Leonard Sachs, Peter Cushing, Derek Griffiths, Syd Lawrence and Ann Hamilton.

With no Johnny Ammonds or Ernest Maxin at Thames, Eric and Ernie found their specials being produced and directed by Keith Beckett. In May 1978, Beckett mentioned Morecambe and Wise during an interview he gave to *Studio News*, Thames Television's in-house magazine. Below is an extract from the article:

> Keith 'Magic Fingers' Beckett has some spectacular plans to bring a new look to Thames' entertainment specials. Here he describes some of his ambitions to *Studio News*.
>
> 'Morecambe and Wise, Harry Secombe, Benny Hill, Tommy Steele – they're all complete professionals. You can't change their styles. You just try and do justice to them,' says producer/director Keith Beckett as he contemplates his projects for 1978.
>
> Already acclaimed as a pioneer of special effects through videotape (last year's *Tommy Steele and a Show* is now up for a Golden Rose of Montreux award), Keith is currently setting up what promise to be some of this year's biggest live entertainment events.
>
> Though the first rehearsals won't begin until August, Morecambe and Wise are already top priority, and are planning their first Thames specials with Keith and their writers Barry Cryer and John Junkin. 'We start rehearsing a full month before the first studio recording, giving us enough time to get every detail absolutely right. These shows will be real humdingers.

'Big guest stars, probably from the film world, will feature alongside Morecambe and Wise. It'll be a show with heart; it won't be a plastic, transatlantic production, it'll be a very British show.

'There's so much enthusiasm, especially from Eric and Ernie. They want to be involved in everything – even the dubbing and editing. There are hundreds of ideas being thrown around. I think for them, it's like starting all over again.'

Development on Morecambe and Wise's specials continues through the year (they'll also be involved in setting up their feature for Euston Films, and the long-awaited guest appearance during the final series of *The Sweeney*…

While the BBC licked its wounds, Eric and Ernie and Thames decided to make light of their defection back to ITV. As their first special started, the double act was shown being supposedly thrown out of a BBC van after being driven to Thames Television's Teddington Studios. The other highlights included Eric and Ernie playing Baloo the Bear and King Louie respectively in a *Jungle Book* routine; a pet-shop sketch that featured Ann Hamilton playing Eric's wife; Donald Sinden acting as the host in a sketch called 'Butler of the Year'; and Judi Dench appearing in a send-up called 'The Story of Dr Jekyll and Mrs Hyde'. Peter Cushing also found himself being blown up by the duo during his attempt to collect his fee for his first ever guest appearance on their show back at the BBC. The special ended with Eric and Ernie performing the song 'Walkin' in the Sunshine'.

During the making of their first special for Thames, Jim Davidson, who was also signed to Thames at the time, was reunited with Eric Morecambe. As previously mentioned, Jim had worked with Eric briefly during a late-night charity matinee in Birmingham. He then came face to face with the comedian again in Norfolk. 'I was appearing at the Wellington Pier Theatre in Great Yarmouth,' said Jim. 'I was walking to my hotel and saw Eric sitting nearby. I said, "Hello Eric!" and he replied, "Hello" and then blanked me, which I thought was strange. Then a year or so later, when I was making *The Jim Davidson Show* in Studio 2 at Thames Television, Morecambe and Wise were in Studio 1 rehearsing a *Jungle Book* sketch for one of their specials. At the pre-record, I was in their studio watching them and Eric saw me standing behind one of the cameras and stopped the rehearsal. I was worried that he was going to throw me out or something. But he walked over to me, shook my hand and told me he was pleased to see me and apologised to me for when we last met. He said it was only after I had gone that he remembered who I was. I thought this was so nice of him and it made me feel ten foot tall!'

Morecambe and Wise's first Christmas show for Thames, entitled *Eric and Ernie's Xmas Show*, was broadcast on Christmas Day 1978. Barry Cryer and John Junkin were once again asked to write the script while Keith Beckett produced and directed the special. Choreography was by Rex Grey and Keith Beckett. The guests in the special included Leonard Rossiter, Frank Finlay, Eamonn Andrews, Nicholas Parsons, Jenny Hanley, Anna Dawson, Jan Hunt, Syd Lawrence and his Orchestra, Jillianne Foot, children from the Italia Conti Stage School and the Mike Sammes Singers.

However, one of the most talked-about guests that year was the former prime minister Harold Wilson, who appeared in one of Eric and Ernie's flat sketches. Eric addressed him as Mike Yarwood at one stage, a reference to Yarwood's popular impressions of the former Labour leader.

A routine in the show attempted to fool viewers into believing that Eric and Ernie were dancing with Anna Ford. Ford had turned down the offer to perform on the show as she feared it would 'seem derivative' after Angela Rippon's 'wonderful dance'. She later admitted, 'I think not appearing on the show is the greatest regret of my life.' It was Denise Gyngell (now Waterman) who doubled for the popular newsreader. 'I was attending Italia Conti School when this golden opportunity arose,' she said. 'I was called to the agency to be told I had been booked to dance with Morecambe and Wise on their next Christmas show. Now, anyone who grew up in the seventies would understand just what a big deal this was. The whole family used to have Christmas lunch and would then sit in front of the television to watch their Christmas special.

'Before I knew it, I was at Thames Television being introduced to the famous pair. They were a lovely couple, charming and friendly. I was particularly impressed with Eric and his natural charm. Rehearsals went ahead and they made it all very easy for me. It didn't take long for the routine to be ready for the cameras.

'On the day we recorded the routine, I went to make-up to be transformed into Anna Ford, then walked out onto the set to strut my stuff with Eric and Ernie. I soon found myself gliding around the studio with the most famous duo in the UK! It wasn't the greatest routine in the world, but then I'm not the greatest dancer, so no surprise there! Whenever the camera got close to my face, I had to make sure I turned my head so people would think I really was Anna Ford.

'After the recording was completed, I remember Eric asking me if I'd like to join them for a bite to eat. I'm not quite sure why, but I declined – was I mad?! A golden opportunity like that and I said no! Looking back, it was one of the most memorable moments in my life, one I will never forget. After all, there's not many people who can boast, "I danced with Morecambe and Wise!"'

Other highlights in the 1978 Christmas special included Leonard Rossiter joining Eric and Ernie in a 'Fabulous Forties' sketch, which culminated in the three performers dressing up as the Andrews Sisters and miming along to their hit 'Boogie Woogie Bugle Boy'. Frank Finlay, meanwhile, found himself being tricked to appear in an Ernest Wise play called *Murder at Nastleigh Grange*.

Another sketch featured Eric and Ernie with a giant Irish wolfhound puppet called Brut. The puppet had previously made a brief appearance in a sketch included in the duo's first special for Thames. John Thirtle and Ian Thom were the two puppeteers who operated Brut. Sadly, John died in 1995, but Ian remembers well his experience of working on these two sketches. 'We were operating the puppet behind the ubiquitous curtains. Eric introduced the dog as Brut adding, "He'll splash it all over you, if you're not careful!" He made the dog (basically just a head, paws and tail) roll over. He then stroked the dog through the curtain. Eric said, "He likes this as well. And I'll tell you something else, the fellow who's stood here likes it as well!" I split the seam on my trousers while were taping the sequence! Eric had lots of stories. He was generally more gregarious than Ernie – but they were both great to work with.'

Around this time, Denise Rayner, who worked at Thames Television's studios on Euston Road, had a brief encounter with Morecambe and Wise when they visited the building. 'I was sat just outside my boss's office,' said Denise. 'The other staff were all whispering, "Morecambe and Wise are walking down the corridor!" I didn't want to stop working on the urgent document I was typing, so I kept my head down. But Eric Morecambe, being Eric Morecambe, suddenly stopped by my desk. I was determined not to let anything distract me. Eventually I wanted to find out what all the "loud silence" was about. I turned my head slowly to the right and as I did Eric plonked a great big kiss on my lips! It was a shock – but a delightful one!'

On 15 March 1979, while opening the fridge at his family home in Harpenden, Eric fell backwards on top of his son, Gary, who was standing nearby. Although he claimed he would 'be all right in a minute,' Eric was suffering a second heart attack. He was taken to St Albans Hospital and was subsequently advised to undergo a heart bypass operation. This was carried out by Magdi Yacoub on 25 June. Had he not taken Yacoub's advice, Eric would have had as little as three months left to live.

The health scares of 1979 left their mental as well as their physical scars. Understandably, Morecambe had to take time to recover after both the heart attack and the subsequent surgery. His wife, Joan, recollected how this period of convalescence affected her husband.

'When Eric was so ill, and then recovering, he couldn't do much. He would go birdwatching; he loved birds and always fed them in the garden. He was devoted to bird life. Eric had a serious side, and the older he got, the more it occurred. He became more philosophical, but he never really lost his sense of humour.'

Eric's son, Gary, has his own views on how his father's second heart attack and heart surgery affected him. 'I saw a huge change in him because he wasn't trying to be so funny at home any more,' he recalled. 'He was cheerful, but he wasn't looking for laughs suddenly. I had lunch with him in London and he wasn't messing around joking with the waiters any more. He was just being a normal customer. I think he'd fallen slightly out of love with comedy, perhaps.' That said, Eric was not against making a witty ad-lib about his second heart attack. As part of a promotional tour to launch Gary's first book about his father, both men appeared on *The Russell Harty Show*. During the on-air conversation, Gary said to Russell, 'With my father's second heart attack, I felt very much a part of it.' Eric then dived in with, 'Yes – he caused it.'

Eric devoted part of 1979 to writing a novel called *Mr Lonely*, while still recovering from heart surgery. The story follows the exploits of a lowly two-bit comedian and womaniser, Sid Lewis, who becomes an overnight success after being spotted by someone from the BBC. Also during his recovery period, Eric spent time fishing with his adopted son, Steven. Away from the pressures of television and live shows, Eric and Steven were able to enjoy some quality time together. 'We didn't have to say anything,' said Steven. 'We just fished in unison. It was just so peaceful. They were good times, special times. With a totally relaxed father.'

To help keep the public updated about Eric's recovery, Ernie gave a magazine interview from his home by the River Thames. Ernie and Doreen had moved to Maidenhead in Berkshire in the early seventies. Wise explained that he had been offered the opportunity to host a television talent show. He also admitted that he had considered what he would do if he and his comedy partner couldn't work together again. Ernie said he was grateful for the modern miracle that saved Eric's life – the open-heart surgery lasting seven hours that followed his second heart attack. He added that he hoped Eric would be fit enough soon to begin a new Christmas special. 'Everyone asks, "How's Eric?" and "Are you going to do a Christmas show?"' he said. 'Well, Eric has grown a moustache and things are easing along. I'm sure everything is going to be all right, but we are not back on the treadmill yet. It's a hard question for him, "Will you be able to do that sort of thing, having had open-heart surgery?" But all I can say is that he seems ready to go.'

Eric become the subject of a portrait painted by artist Richard Stone in 1979. 'Anglia Television had been keen to make a prime-time documentary of my artistic journey from postman's son to, apparently, a favourite Court artist,' said Richard. 'However, they were somewhat at a loss as to who would be a suitable subject for me to paint for the programme. An Anglia Television executive suggested that he would ask his friend Eric Morecambe if there was any possibility that he would subject himself to the scrutiny not only of the television camera, but also of an almost unknown young artist.

'After an initial meeting with me at his home in Harpenden, Eric agreed to give it a go. A series of sittings were booked, and a studio hired in a disused warehouse overlooking Tower Bridge. The filming of *Morecambe and Stone* was an incredibly enjoyable experience. Eric's spontaneous joking, his reminiscences of his childhood days on stage and the insight into the influences shaping his comic genius were fascinating.

'Eric was happy to participate in the film for no fee other than the portrait itself, if he liked it. However, there was to be one proviso. As the credits rolled over his portrait at the end of the film, he insisted on adding a "d" to the end of my surname. This was a final comic touch that didn't remain on the picture for posterity.'

The programme ended with the painting being unveiled at a party attended by Eric and fellow performers, including Lenny Henry. When he was a fledgling comedian in the late seventies, Lenny worked supporting Eric and Ernie during one of their 'bank raids' at a theatre in Bournemouth. He never forgot the kindness that Eric showed him. Lenny went on in the first half and was supposed to perform for just twelve minutes. However, the audience laughed so much that the Dudley-born comedian stayed on for seventeen minutes. This resulted in the stage manager giving him a telling-off for running over. Eric witnessed this exchange and told Lenny not to worry, and that he thought he was brilliant. Indeed, he encouraged him to perform for the same amount of time the following evening. Morecambe also encouraged Lenny to use his dressing room and partake in the beer that had originally been provided for him.

It would have been understandable if, given Eric's health, there had been no new television shows made by Morecambe and Wise in 1979. Unbelievably, Eric managed to get before the cameras with Ernie again at Teddington for a programme called *Eric and Ernie's Christmas*. Admittedly, their workload was cut to make delivering a special more bearable for Morecambe. The sixty-minute programme saw the double act reunited with their former scriptwriter Eddie Braben and producer and director Johnny Ammonds. Ammonds shared the directing duties with Keith Beckett. The format mainly consisted of the boys being interviewed by David Frost, with Des O'Connor and Glenda Jackson also joining in the conversation. Additionally, there were appearances from Garfield Morgan, Janet Webb and Arthur Tolcher.

The special also featured a handful of sketches. They included Eric and Ernie and Glenda Jackson performing the song 'Side by Side' while sitting next to each other on chairs. During the number, Jackson's chair was raised and lowered while, naturally, the double act's chairs remained in place. The duo had previously performed this sketch with Roy Castle over at the BBC. On that occasion, Eric was the victim who found himself being raised and lowered. Another sketch saw Eric and Ernie playing Sylvester the Cat and Tweety Bird (sometimes known as Tweety Pie) respectively in a sketch that saw them miming to the song 'I Tawt I Taw a Puddy Tat'. The sketch included another appearance by the Irish wolfhound puppet, Brut.

In 1980, Eric played the Funny Uncle in a dramatisation of the poem 'Indoor Games in Newbury' as part of *Betjeman's Britain* for Anglia Television. Produced and directed by Charles Wallace, the programme was based on the works of writer John Betjeman. The other performers in this production included Peter Cook, Madeline Smith, Susannah York, Lyn McCarthy, Brad Clayton, Caroline Langrishe and John Betjeman.

The first series of *The Morecambe and Wise Show* for Thames was taped at Teddington in 1980. This was Eric and Ernie's first television series since 1976. The six thirty-minute editions, which ran weekly from 3 September until 8 October, were written by Eddie Braben and produced and directed by Johnny Ammonds. The guests included Terry Wogan, Hannah Gordon, Hugh Paddick, Dave Prowse, Deryck Guyler, Suzanne Danielle, Tessa Wyatt and Gemma Craven. As with most of their work for Thames, this series included a lot of reworked material. Probably the most obvious for viewers would have been the opening spot in edition six in which Eric played Mr Fantastic. This was to all intents and purposes a restaging of the famous 'Mr Memory' sketch they recorded for one of their BBC shows in 1973.

There were certainly many highlights of the series. They included a flat sketch in the fifth edition in which Suzanne Danielle pretended to be a fellow writer like 'Little Ern'. The sketch included a non-speaking cameo appearance from Tessa Wyatt, who was playing Richard O'Sullivan's partner in the Thames sitcom *Robin's Nest* at the time.

In the sixth edition of their first series for Thames, Gemma Craven (best known for playing Cinderella in Bryan Forbes's film *The Slipper and the Rose*) played Ernie's sexy French maid called Michelle in another flat-based sketch. Craven also played Cyd Charisse to Ernie's Gene Kelly in a parody of the 'Broadway Melody' ballet from musical *Singin' in the Rain*. At one point, Eric, dressed in his famous flat cap and coat, manages to upstage the couple by being raised into the studio roof.

Eric and Ernie were back with *The Morecambe and Wise Christmas Show* on Christmas Day 1980. The sixty-minute special was written by Eddie Braben and produced and directed by Johnny Ammonds. The guests joining the double act for their festive offering that year included Peter Barkworth, Glenda Jackson, Jill Gascoine, Hannah Gordon, Peter Cushing, Alec Guinness and Mick McManus. In this special, Eric and Ernie played carol singers in a series of sketches supposedly set outside Number 10, Downing Street. In attempting to get a large donation in their collecting tin from Margaret Thatcher, the pair find themselves being tricked by Peter Cushing into finally paying them his long-overdue fee!

Other high spots included Jill Gascoine, who was playing Maggie Forbes in LWT's police series *The Gentle Touch* at the time, joining Eric and Ernie for Christmas lunch in another of their flat sketches. It's interesting to note that the flat sketch element would also become used by Cannon and Ball and by Hale and Pace at various times in their long-running shows made by LWT.

It could be argued that the finest sketch in the 1980 Christmas special was Ern's version of *Hamlet* – written with the aid of Eddie Braben, of course! In addition to Morecambe and Wise, the send-up included guest appearances from Hannah Gordon and Peter Barkworth. Although Hannah had worked with Eric and Ernie on two previous occasions, this was Peter's first time. However, the two guests had worked together before when they played husband and wife in the BBC drama series *Telford's Change* the previous year.

Hannah believes the double act couldn't have achieved what they did without all the experience they had gained in their early years in the business. 'They served a wonderful apprenticeship,' she said. 'They were such a team. I learnt so much from them.' She has blissful memories of her time on the 1980 special. 'We had such a good time that I remember saying to Peter, "Can you believe we're getting paid for this?!"'

As already indicated, Morecambe and Wise treated all their guests well off-camera. Further proof was given by Jan Clennell, a dancer on one of their Thames shows. 'The rehearsal period was fun and light-hearted,' she said, 'but very professional when we were practising the dance numbers. Both Eric and Ernie respected us dancers; they sat with us and we all ate lunch together and I felt included in their chats. That was very special.'

Eric's first novel, *Mr Lonely*, was finally published for the first time in 1981. The book received praise by the critics. While he may have been tempted to step away from television and become a full-time writer, Eric never did make the break. It was true that working in television had taken its toll, and maybe he had lost his appetite for comedy. However, he felt a sense of loyalty to Ernie and the double act, and this was argu-ably the main reason for not making a drastic change to his professional life.

But despite never walking away from the Morecambe and Wise brand, Eric did take on further projects that saw him working without Wise. Indeed, following the success of *Betjeman's Britain*, producer and director Charles Wallace cast Eric as Major Maxton-Weir in a short film called *Later Flowering Love* for Paramount Pictures. The other members of the cast included John Betjeman (who acted as the narrator), Susannah York, Beryl Reid, John Alderton, Jenny Agutter and John Le Mesurier. The film was released in cinemas in the UK with *Indiana Jones and the Raiders of the Lost Ark*.

Ernie and Glenda Jackson were reunited again in 1981 – but this time without Eric. They were brought together to appear in an entertaining public inform-ation film designed to recruit blood donors. 'You told me you'd take me to Hollywood!' exclaims Glenda in this three-minute film. 'No, Cricklewood,' replies

Ernie. It still raises a smile and puts across an important message when viewed all these years later.

Morecambe and Wise were back in the studio in 1981 to make their second series for Thames. This time they made seven editions. These were broadcast weekly from 1 September until 13 October 1981. Eddie Braben once again wrote the scripts and Johnny Ammonds produced and directed the thirty-minute shows. The guests during this series included Gemma Craven, Richard Vernon, Max Bygraves, Diane Keen, Hannah Gordon, Richard Chisholm, Peter Bowles, Suzanne Danielle, Robert Hardy, Ian Ogilvy and Joanna Lumley. The highlights included Eric, Ernie and Suzanne Danielle giving a rousing rendition of 'All That Jazz' from the musical *Chicago*. Joanna Lumley appeared in Ernie's version of *The Barretts of Wimpole Street*; and Lumley and the duo also performed 'Thoroughly Modern Millie' from the musical of the same name.

As mentioned, the actress Diane Keen had briefly appeared with Morecambe and Wise on one of their television shows at the BBC before she became well known. Since then, she had gone on to play lead roles in programmes including *The Cuckoo Waltz*, *Rings on Their Fingers* and *Shillingbury Tales*. 'I was in New York when my agent called and asked if I would appear with Morecambe and Wise again,' explained Diane. 'When I went to the first rehearsal, I was very tired because I had just flown back to London and had jet lag. I drank lots of coffee to keep awake. Because Eric knew I was very tired, I kept hearing him asking Ernie if I was still awake!

'When they were working together, they functioned as one. But I remember them telling me that they didn't see each other or socialise when they weren't working.

'Eric was right up front about his heart surgery. When we were having coffee, he told me all about his operation and showed me his scars. He cracked lots of jokes while we were rehearsing. I am not sure, but I think it helped him get into the right mood for working and being funny.

'Eric and Ernie were a joy to work with. After we'd made the show, I gave them both a bottle of port each to thank them for all the fun we'd had. They were thrilled and told me that none of their other guests had ever done anything like that for them before.

'After Eric died, I met Ernie at the Hampton Court Flower Show. It was on a day before it was opened to the public. Ernie came over to me and said, "I don't know if you remember, but you were a guest on our show." I said, "Are you kidding me?! Of course I remember!" We sat and talked about the show and looked around the gardens together. He seemed very lost without Eric. Sadly, I never saw him again.'

While Christmas 1981 saw Morecambe and Wise appear in another Christmas special, this time called

Eric and Ernie's Christmas Show, the programme wasn't broadcast on Christmas Day as usual. Instead, it was broadcast on 23 December. At the time, LWT (London Weekend Television) were the ITV franchise-holders at weekends, broadcasting from Friday evening until Monday morning. Because Christmas Day fell on a Friday that year, naturally LWT's programmes were shown and not those made by Thames. This must have irked the pair somewhat, as Eric made a reference to this schedule change in one of the sketches in the show.

Producer and director Johnny Ammonds had put together a pleasing cast for the Christmas special that year. The guests included Ralph Richardson, Robert Hardy, Ian Ogilvy, Susannah York, Alvin Stardust and Suzanne Danielle. The script was once again written by Eddie Braben. One of the biggest highlights that year was Ian Ogilvy and Susannah York appearing in Ernie's version of *Julius Caesar*, bringing back memories of Morecambe and Wise's version of *Antony and Cleopatra* at the BBC.

In 1982, Eric wrote the first of two children's novels, *The Reluctant Vampire*. The story, aimed at readers aged seven and eight, featured an extremely unconventional vampire who preferred chips and a glass of red wine to blood!

Having struck up a friendship while working together on *Betjeman's Britain* and *Late Flowering Love*, Eric agreed to appear in Charles Wallace's new comedy film, *The Passionate Pilgrim*. Eric made only two stipulations in his film work with Wallace: they must not do anything that conflicted with Morecambe and Wise; and, in the stories, Eric always had to get the girl! The cast of *The Passionate Pilgrim*, which was made entirely on location at Hever Castle, also featured Tom Baker and Madeline Smith, with John Le Mesurier as the narrator. The story concerns a lord (Eric) and his lady (Madeline Smith), with the latter attracting the amorous attentions of the titular character (played by Tom Baker). The plot centres on the pilgrim's failed attempts to gain entry to the castle by any means possible, and the lengths the lord will go to in order to stop him.

Madeline Smith, who had worked with Eric and Charles before on *Betjeman's Britain*, was very pleased to be asked to appear in this new short film. 'I was just about to start college full-time when we began,' she recalled. 'I remember thinking what a wonderful swan-song from acting it was to be working with Eric Morecambe!

'When we started filming in October 1982, Eric was showing signs of fatigue. Tom Baker used to keep him up so late talking, and I was so worried about him. But when Eric had an audience, he was unstoppable.

'Eric had no airs at all. We spoke like old friends when we were filming at Hever Castle. He was a humble and modest man. Fame had not gone to his head at all and he was a sweetheart to me.

'He loved doing the film and put his heart and soul into it. Eric loved to work, and worked himself very hard rehearsing "pratfalls" for the film.

'For part of the filming, it was chilly and damp and for at least some of the shots I can remember the make-up lady standing with an umbrella over Eric and me!

'Eric was valiant – a real soldier. He fought on, putting his life on the line, quite literally, to bring everything he could to his part in *The Passionate Pilgrim*. Despite his health problems, he never ever complained, but was concerned for my well-being, because we worked so hard.

'I totally adored Eric and I can say that with my hand on my heart. He was so funny in real life – a genuinely funny man. What an inspiration to me he was.

'I owe so much to the director Charles Wallace for giving me two dream jobs.'

When shooting of the initial scenes was over, Charles Wallace became convinced he could add extra material to the film, but these plans were initially put on hold.

10

The End of an Era

URING HIS TIME AT THAMES Television, Eric and some of the production team members from *The Morecambe and Wise Show* would sit and have a drink with Benny Hill and his producer and director, Dennis Kirkland, at lunchtime. Dennis witnessed the nervous energy that Eric would often display while considering the sketch or song-and-dance routine he and Ernie were working on at the time.

Eric would say to Benny, 'It's all based on fear, Ben;' while Thames's biggest star would reply, 'Fingernails and aspirins!' The comedians would then discuss with great concern how their respective series were going overall.

Despite being two of the most successful men in British comedy history, their lack of confidence in their own abilities and talents could still come to the surface in the company of those they trusted. Even once another show had been successfully committed to tape, Eric and Ernie would be quick to conduct an inquest up in the bar at Thames. Questions such as, 'Could we have done that bit better?' and 'Is there any chance of doing that again?' would fill the room.

Kirkland saw at first hand the comedown that Eric and other comedians experienced. 'The euphoria with people like that lasted for minutes,' he said. 'Eric Morecambe was one of the funniest men we ever presented to the world, and yet people don't understand that there was tension behind it all – and nor should they. All they want is their hero on the telly.'

Series three of *The Morecambe and Wise Show* for Thames began its seven-week run on 27 October 1982 and ran until 8 December 1982. Eddie Braben and Johnny Ammonds were once again on scriptwriting and producing and directing duties respectively. The guests in the series included Richard Briers, Diana Dors, Bonnie Langford, Trevor Eve, Wayne Sleep, Jimmy Young, Roy Castle, Colin Welland, Isla St Clair, Nigel Hawthorne and Patricia Brake. Highlights of this series included Eric and Ernie appearing with Richard Briers and Diana Dors in a play called *Captain Blood*. The duo also performed alongside Roy Castle in a sketch based around the song 'Copacabana'.

Christmas 1982 saw Morecambe and Wise appear in *Eric and Ernie's Xmas Show* for Thames. Yet again, this special was not broadcast on Christmas Day; in fact, it wasn't shown until 27 December. The sixty-minute programme was written by Eddie Braben and produced and directed by Johnny Ammonds. This would mark the last time that Ammonds would work with Morecambe and Wise. Robert Hardy, Rula Lenska, Richard Vernon and Wall Street Crash were just some of the guests who left their egos at the door and proved themselves to be good sports. This festive edition saw Eric and Ernie add a comical element to Wall Street Crash's version of 'Alexander's Ragtime Band', while Rula Lenska appeared in Ernie's latest play, *Yukon Gold Rush*.

The dawning of 1983 would, without anyone realising it, mark the start of Morecambe and Wise's last full year together. It began with them appearing in a one-hour special for Thames called *Eric and Ernie's Variety Days*. Broadcast on 2 March 1983, it consisted of the double act reminiscing about their days performing in variety. The year would see Eric take another break from his day job and once again put pen to paper. In doing so, he wrote and published the second of his two novels designed for children, *The Vampire's Revenge*. Morecambe set the comical tale in the small town of

Katchem-by-the-Throat, in the tiny country of Gotcha. It was there that Prince Vernon Vampire was out to seek a terrible revenge.

The fourth and final ever series of *The Morecambe and Wise Show* began on 7 September 1983. The six editions ran weekly until 19 October. Although Eddie Braben once again wrote the scripts, it was down to Mark Stuart to produce and direct the programmes. Margaret Courtenay, David Kernan, Stutz Bear Cats and Harry Fowler all made guest appearances during the series. As with other programmes Eric and Ernie made for Thames, there was a familiar theme to some of the sketches and routines in this series. The double act even performed an updated version of their classic 'Swiss Slapping Dance'. The 'Mr Bartholomew the Pigeon Fancier' sketch was, however, new and is often shown when Morecambe and Wise's Thames era is mentioned on television. Eric played the said pigeon fancier, using his real second name, and Ernie played a reporter from Thames Television. During the sketch, a pigeon lands in a bucket with a message from the other side:

Reporter:	Oh look, it's got a message on its legs.
Mr Bartholomew:	It's one I've been expecting.
Reporter:	Who's it from?
Mr Bartholomew:	It's from the BBC.
Reporter:	Really?
Mr Bartholomew:	'Come home boys, all is forgiven.'

A chance to make a new film was one of the reasons that Morecambe and Wise made the switch to Thames. However, this project had still not materialised. What type of film had originally been discussed is not known. Finally, a television film called *Night Train to Murder*, which was written and directed by Joseph McGrath, was green-lit. In addition to Eric and Ernie, the cast included Margaret Courtenay, Kenneth Haigh, Fulton Mackay, Pamela Salem, Lysette Anthony, Roger Brierley, Edward Judd, Ben Aris and Richard Vernon.

Morecambe and Wise essentially acted as a version of themselves in this film – even to the point of playing a double act touring in variety. Although the film opened with Eric and Ernie standing at the graveside of a cast member who had supposedly died during production, the story was set in 1946. After breaking the fourth wall and introducing the film, the murder mystery begins, and a host of characters die in strange circumstances.

The production was taped in Studio 2 at Thames Television Studios in Teddington, while locations used in the film included Sheffield Park Station on the Bluebell Railway in East Sussex and Albury Park Mansion in Albury Park, Guildford, Surrey. The house and grounds have since been used for the filming of the ITV drama series *Midsomer Murders*.

'Meeting Eric Morecambe is my best memory of the whole film,' revealed Pamela Salem, who played Cousin

Zelda. 'He was a wonderful human being. I cannot praise him too highly. He was even funnier off-screen than on. He was a naturally generous and kind-hearted person, who had time for everyone, an enthusiasm for life, and personally I feel privileged to have met him.

'When I first interviewed for my part in the film, I reminded Eric that my husband, Michael O'Hagan, had acted with him twenty years previously in panto; and at that time, Eric, as a surprise, had given dinner jackets to him and the property master, so they could go to the black-tie charity affair to which they had been invited. Eric had tucked money into their pockets so they could buy drinks and hold their own at the Comedians' Table. Eric remembered Michael, and when I told him he had driven me to the interview, he jumped up and insisted Michael came in. After all those years he still had time for his mates.

'I used to try and spend as much time with Eric off stage as on because he was such an interesting and humorous man; he came at life from such a refreshing and insightful angle, and he made me laugh when we acted together.

'Unfortunately, I did not think the script for *Night Train to Murder* was funny, and I was worried that our scenes would not work. When I voiced my concerns to anyone, I was told that this was light entertainment and Joe would get it together in the editing. I did not feel at all happy doing the film, although I was delighted to meet up with the truly gifted Kenneth Haigh again, and we had an excellent cast. Lysette Anthony was one of the most beautiful girls you could hope to see, but even with such a good cast the film did not work. At the time, I had not worked in light entertainment and so I thought it must be my inexperience that made me so anxious, but unfortunately my instincts were correct. Nothing is wasted, however, and I learned a lot, including to trust my own instincts; and I had the joy of meeting and spending time with Eric Morecambe. I also got to keep a beautifully comfortable pair of high shoes that were made for me!

'The cast and crew socialised together in the bar at Thames Television in Teddington. It was always one of the favourite places to work as it was situated on a beautiful spot on the River Thames, and everyone treated you very well. I don't know how we lunched in the bar in those days and then went to do an afternoon's work! My method is much more disciplined these days but then I am a lot older and, I hope, wiser!'

Early in the film's story, Morecambe and Wise can be seen performing a routine set to the song 'I'll Buy That Dream'. The double act is supposedly playing a variety theatre in Carlisle as part of a tour. Zoe Nicholas played one of the soubrettes backing the duo in this sequence. 'Eric and Ernie were so lovely to me,' she said. 'They were very friendly and put me at ease as I was nervous. Eric kept making me laugh and I remember him giving me sweets. They were charming and I treasure having met them.'

Peter Willcocks was a sound supervisor at Thames Television at the time that Morecambe and Wise were making *Night Train to Murder*. 'The production was made using the usual equipment, but in the style of a film shoot in many ways, with Joe McGrath working on the studio floor most of the time. My colleague, Paul Gartrell, also worked on the sound for the film. There was a running gag about Ernie having a crick in his neck when he turned it to one side. He added the most excruciating multiple knuckle crunch to the track, which made all those at the dub laugh a lot. At the end of the day, everyone was rubbing their necks!'

Christmas 1983 saw what was fated to be Morecambe and Wise's last Christmas show and the last show they made together. Appropriately titled *Eric and Ernie's Christmas Show*, it was broadcast on Boxing Day. In addition to material written by Eddie Braben, a custard pie routine and a stools routine written by Sid Green and Dick Hills were used again in this special. The latter was played out as the end credits rolled. It involved Eric and Ernie performing 'Swingin' Down the Lane', a song usually performed by Frank Sinatra, with a stool each as a prop. Eric's stool supposedly had glue spread on the top. This resulted in him getting stuck to Ernie's dinner-suit tails while trying to perform the routine.

The last Christmas special was produced and directed by Mark Stuart and choreographed by Norman Maen. Morecambe and Wise's guests included Gemma Craven, Nigel Hawthorne, Derek Jacobi, Burt Kwouk, Fulton Mackay, Tony Monopoly, Patrick Mower, Nanette Newman, Peter Skellern, Stutz Bear Cats and the Thames Television continuity announcer, Philip Elsmore.

Had it not been for the determination of Eric Morecambe, this programme may never have been completed, as Gemma Craven still remembers. 'We did a *Mack and Mabel* "Keystone Cops" sequence with Eric and Ernie both dressed as policemen,' she said. 'I was at the top of this ladder. One minute I could see both Eric and Ernie below, the next I could only see Ernie. Eric had collapsed and the paramedics had to take him to hospital. When Eric got better, he came back and, bless him, finished the show. I greatly admired him for that. He came back and carried on as if nothing had happened. I remember him saying, "Anything to give you a tea break!" They broke the mould when they made him. He was a one-off, a consummate professional, and I loved him so much.'

Discussing Morecambe and Wise reminded Gemma of a musical number she agreed to do for the duo. 'I had to jump into a tank of water. I am terrified of water! However, I jumped in. It was only four feet deep – but I had to go under the water. I was really scared. I didn't tell them until afterwards. Eric loved that and gave me a big hug and burst out laughing. They then told me that no one else would agree to do it!'

Susan Colclough was a member of the vocal harmony group Stutz Bear Cats when the call came to appear with Eric and Ernie. But while some guests just appeared once or twice, Susan was far luckier. 'I worked with Morecambe and Wise three times,' she enthused. 'We performed on two shows in their last series and on their final Christmas show. In those days, we had the luxury of two weeks' rehearsal for the production numbers alone, so we worked closely with Eric and Ernie for all that time. It was an honour and a joy.

'I remember having a bond with Eric as I was born and bred in Fleetwood, which is close to his home town of Morecambe, so we chatted about the places we both knew up there. He mentioned Grime's, a well-known pie shop in Fleetwood, and he remembered how he loved their pies. I joked, "I'll get my Mum to send some," and he replied, "If your Mum sends pies from Grime's, you can do another show in the series." I told Mum – and she sent them! The next day, I presented them to Eric, who was astonished and delighted – and sure enough we did get a second show in that series. The exact same thing happened with shrimps from a fish shop in Morecambe, when, even more surprised to be presented with his favourite shrimps, Eric promised us a slot on their Christmas special! I'm sure it wasn't just down to the pies and shrimps; but I reckon it helped!'

Susan witnessed at first hand how Eric coped admirably if things didn't go quite to plan during the making of a show. 'I remember Eric's total professionalism, during the filming of the second programme we did with them, when a prop didn't work. Clearly, this was a disaster considering all the rehearsing, and the cost involved, but Eric very calmly and politely said simply, "Well, we'll change it," and immediately came up with a Luton Town FC gag (in the middle of an Oriental number!), which worked.'

Susan found herself falling victim to one of Eric's famous practical jokes while she was working with the double act. 'The staff bar at Thames Television in Teddington was long and quite narrow,' she explained. 'The entrance was at the bar end, with a private function room way down at the other end with glass walls and glass door. One evening, while working on the Christmas special, we were walking toward the bar entrance and Eric was ahead of us. He turned and waited for us to catch up, and silently put his elbow out for me to link it. I duly did (sort of waiting for a funny line – but none came). He escorted me into the bar and carried on walking towards the private function room at the other end. He silently, and with due purpose, walked with a large swagger. Everyone was watching us (with amusement!) during this quite long walk through the entire length of the bar. It was obvious that a posh private function for the executives at Thames was being held in the room ahead, and the thoughts going through my mind included "Have we been invited and someone has forgotten to tell me?" and "I wish I'd dressed appropriately for this."

'Eric opened the door into the function, encouraging me to walk in, making sure that everyone inside stopped their conversation to look at us making an entrance (we clearly hadn't been invited!). When I was safely inside, standing alone, Eric said very loudly, "I'll pick you up in half an hour love," and left closing the door behind him! Everyone (including me!) roared with laughter, then he reopened the door and let me out. It is one of my funniest memories of him.

'Apart, that is, from our final day of filming when I was stranded at the studios without transport to Richmond Station, and Eric kindly offered to drop me off. He parked directly outside the station, which was very crowded with busy commuters. I thanked Eric, and quickly left the car to head towards the station. As I walked toward the entrance, he got out of the car, for all to see him, and shouted, "And bring back that frying pan!" Again, everyone around laughed; including him – he'd made everyone's day!

'Eric really was as funny off-screen as he was on. He was one of the nicest men in show business, and working with Morecambe and Wise is up there as one of the true highlights of my career.'

To this day, Susan treasures the following letter she received from Eric:

Heartburn Hotel,
Herts.
Dear Sue,

Thank you for the 'Hope You're Soon Well and Swinging Again' card; I loved the picture of Mark Stuart on the front. I realise that people like me don't grow on trees… they swing from them… is that what you were trying to say on your card? We did the show the other night and it went very well. The best bit in it was when I walked forward and introduced you as 'The Stuffed Bear Cats'; it was taken out. Then I called you 'The Stutz Beer Cans', that was also taken out. Then I called your agent – and she took me out!

Tell your mother not to worry about the shrimps; they had nothing to do with my little heart flutter, it was the black puddings. My lawyer will be in touch after Christmas. Please remember me to the boys, all three of them; why that pretty one calls himself Jane I'll never know.

See you soon,
Love, Eric

With the Christmas special in the can, Eric and Ernie could relax. Gone were the days when they appeared together in pantomime, complete with a hectic performing schedule.

The start of 1984 saw *Night Train to Murder* being edited at Thames. When Eric was shown the final cut, he was not pleased. 'It was so dated, and Eric was bitterly disappointed,' said Eric's wife, Joan. 'He thought they were going to come out with something fresh. He was really very disappointed in that.'

Morecambe's daughter, Gail, agrees that the film was not the happiest of experiences for her father. 'When I watched the film, I didn't really take it in,' she admitted. 'I was more preoccupied thinking that Dad didn't look too well. When he saw it, he was shocked and didn't want anyone else to see it.' At Eric's request, *Night Train to Murder* was shelved by Thames. However, the film would eventually find its way onto television screens.

The year 1984 also saw Eric write *Eric Morecambe on Fishing*. The book, which was illustrated by David Hughes, included a special foreword written by Ernie Wise. Wise admitted that he couldn't understand how anyone could enjoy spending all day on a riverbank in the cold and rain – despite not even catching a single fish! In the publication, Eric charted his lifelong love of fishing, from fishing trips with his father to the ups and downs of owing his own fish in aquariums at his Harpenden home.

On 7 April 1984, Eric appeared as a guest on *The Saturday Show*, a live Saturday-morning children's show made by Central Television at their then Birmingham base. It was hosted by Tommy Boyd and Isla St Clair, with Jeremy Beadle sometimes assisting. One of the photos taken during the broadcast shows Eric sitting with the children and a cardboard cut-out of Des O'Connor in the audience!

On 18 April 1984, Eric appeared on TV-am. He was interviewed by his friend and fellow Luton FC fan, Nick Owen. 'Eric was in sparkling form,' he said. 'I hosted the show alongside my friend John Stapleton. (Anne Diamond was on a day off, much to her chagrin!) At one stage, we checked that he was all right to stay with us for a bit longer. "Stay?" he said. "I could marry you!" He told us he had three children, but he wasn't sure because he'd left home early that day. Luton had played West Ham the night before. I knew he hadn't been there, so I brought him a programme and handed it to him on air. He said, "Thanks, I'll treasure that," and then tossed it over his shoulder onto the rubber plants. We covered various subjects, including his health. He said how grateful he was for the bypass surgery he had had after suffering heart attacks in 1968 and 1979. He felt as fit as ever, he said, and he looked really well.'

Thames Television, in association with Mark Goodson Productions and Talbot Television, brought the panel show *What's My Line?* back to the nation's screens on 26 March 1984. Previously, the UK versions had been made and shown by the BBC. Eamonn Andrews, who had presented the very first BBC version between 1951 and 1963, was again at the helm of the programme. Eric appeared as a panellist a total of four times during this series. On an edition broadcast on 23 April 1984 (listed as VTR 29810 in FremantleMedia's archive), Ernie appeared as the mystery celebrity guest. While very few people remember this edition of the programme, its place in the history of Morecambe and Wise is incredibly important. Put simply, it marked the last time Eric and Ernie appeared on television together.

Invented by Eamonn Andrews, *Whose Baby?* was a Thames Television panel game show that ran at various times between 1973 and 1988. By 1984, Bernie Winters was the host of the series. The basic premise of the show was that a celebrity panel, which during its lifetime included the likes of Nanette Newman and Kenneth Williams, would meet members of a celebrity's family and try and guess who their famous father and mother were. Not surprisingly, and with Eric under contract to Thames, the production team felt that one half of Morecambe and Wise would be a perfect subject for the show. Gail, Eric's daughter, was elected to guest on the show with her two children. And despite being ill and having a high temperature, Gail looked calm, collected and a real credit to her father as she sat on the sofa and faced the panel. The edition's other celebrity guests included The Nolans, Leslie Thomas and Bill Owen. With the edition of *Whose Baby?* successfully taped, the programme was edited and was put on the shelf ready for broadcast.

Morecambe and Wise's old friend Stan Stennett had contacted Eric at the start of 1984 to see if he would take part in an interview about his life. He agreed, and the date for the show was set for Sunday 27 May 1984 at the Roses Theatre in Tewkesbury, Gloucestershire. This would be just thirteen days after his fifty-eighth birthday. 'He arrived about four o'clock in the afternoon,' Stan recalled. 'We didn't start the show until seven o'clock. He came in and put his arms around me and said, "How long did you want me to do boss?" We laughed about that and he laughed with the cleaners and with the people getting the scenery ready. He spent half the evening in the dressing room just talking to the rest of the pros. He didn't want a room on his own, he wanted to go in with the rest of the acts on the bill. We spent the second half of the show doing a little bit of chat, like a *Parkinson* type of interview. We talked about the old days, about the gags we did and so on.'

Tommy Cooper collapsed from a heart attack while appearing on stage in LWT's *Live from Her Majesty's*, which was shown live by ITV on 15 April 1984. He was pronounced dead on arrival at Westminster Hospital. While onstage at the Roses Theatre, Stan Stennett and Eric discussed Cooper's passing. 'Eric said, "Well I wouldn't like to die on stage." I said as a quick retort, "I've died on stage many times." It was flippant in its own way.' Gary, Eric's son, who wasn't present at the theatre, said, 'Stan took him right back over his life and my mother said Eric came out with things she didn't even know about. It was like this final surge, blurting everything out about his life, really developing his answers in full.' Eric told the audience that he was 'proud to have undergone open-heart surgery and grateful for the extra years he won'. After the interview ended, and Morecambe had first left the stage, the musicians returned and picked up their instruments. Stan Stennett led his band in a musical tribute to Eric. The comedian rushed back onto the stage to join them and played various instruments, making six curtain calls. 'We played "The Entertainer" and Eric went around all the instruments just doing a little bit of this and a little bit of that,' explained Stennett. 'Then he went off to his little "Bring Me Sunshine" dance.'

All might have been going well on stage, but in her seat in the auditorium, Eric's wife was starting to worry.

'I think, in a way, that was what killed him when he worked at Tewkesbury. I sat there petrified. I knew he had to get off that stage. They were so thrilled to have him there, and the other people on the show had come on and joined Eric at the end, but he couldn't get off and kept taking these bows. The band had all started up and he couldn't get off the stage. And I knew he had to. I could tell that he was on such a high with the adrenaline, what with all this activity.' According to Eric's chauffeur, Mike Fountain, Eric finally walked into the wings of the theatre and said, 'Thank God that's over.' He then had what turned out to be a third and fatal heart attack and hit his head on a weight at the side of the stage.

Eric was rushed to Cheltenham General Hospital, where he died just before 4.00am on 28 May 1984. At 7.20am, Ernie, heavily in shock, was interviewed by John Stapleton on TV-am. Wise explained that Stan Stennett had originally asked both him and Eric to take part in separate interviews at the Roses Theatre in Tewkesbury. It had been agreed that Eric would do the first interview and Ernie the second. Asked if he thought on reflection Eric should have quit the business, Ernie replied, 'I don't think he could have done that. I don't think he would have been happy taking it easy. But what he was trying to find was something that didn't carry the stress. Something that was easy to do.

That's why he was doing things like *What's My Line?* and *Looks Familiar*. Programmes where you just sit there and reminisce and think back and make jokes.' Ernie later added, 'He was a natural comedian and I was very proud to be his partner. He was a great comedian, and through the years I think they'll realise what a great comedian he was.' At the end of the interview, John Stapleton tentatively broached the subject of Ernie's future. 'I won't give up show business, but it won't be the same.'

For Eric's daughter, Gail, it was almost as if her father had realised his time was short. 'On the Saturday before he died on the Monday, the family went to a wedding in Harpenden,' she recalled. 'In the morning, Dad came through the kitchen door. He looked at me and I had a feeling something was wrong. He didn't look well. Dad and I used to communicate on two levels – I used to get the feeling that we can function on two levels. With Dad, there seemed to be an everyday self and then someone who had a sixth sense about it all. For instance, towards the end, he had cleared out drawers and put various things in order. Dad sat next to me in church on the Saturday and held my hand all the way through the service. Then the following week I was sat in the same pew in the church for his funeral looking at his coffin. I remember that Mike Fountain, Dad's chauffeur, called at around four in the morning to tell me that Dad had collapsed after the show in Tewkesbury. Then I had a phone call later to say that he had died. I know his heart couldn't cope with any more. But I was still shocked.'

Glenda Jackson was one of the many performers who paid tribute to Eric after the news was announced. She recalled her memories of working on the first show she appeared on with the double act. 'My clearest memory is of truly rolling on the floor with laughing,' she said. 'I left that rehearsal room and my ribs ached because I'd done nothing but laugh all day. But they worked extremely hard. They were hugely professional, very helpful, and when you did their shows it was really like a holiday with pay because they would never have allowed you either to have made a disastrous mistake or to have done something that would have made you look an unlikeable fool in the eyes of the public.'

In a change to their schedule, ITV broadcast *Bring Me Sunshine: A Tribute to Eric Morecambe* on the evening of 28 May 1984. The programme, made by Thames Television, featured Michael Parkinson, Ernie Wise and Des O'Connor reminiscing about the late comedian.

Eric's funeral was held on 4 June 1984 at St Nicholas Church, Harpenden. Many performers from the world of show business attended to pay their respects. They included Ronnie Barker, Janet Brown, Roy Castle, Ronnie Corbett, Leslie Crowther, Barry Cryer, Suzanne

Danielle, Bruce Forsyth, Robert Hardy, Patrick Mower, Nicholas Parsons, Robert Powell, Stan Stennett and Norman Vaughan. Eric's daughter, Gail, has an abiding memory of one of the floral tributes. 'I remember the comedian Benny Hill sent a huge arrangement of sweet peas to the funeral,' she said. 'He couldn't attend, because I think he was away in the south of France.'

The principal address was delivered, at Eric's request, by Dickie Henderson. In the summer of 1984, Henderson explained how he came to be asked. 'When my very dear friend, well everyone's dear friend, Arthur Askey left us, at the memorial service I was asked to give the address, and Eric was there. A couple of days later I got this letter from Eric.'

> Dear Dickie,
>
> I very rarely write to famous people – that's why I am writing to you! I would just like to say that I thought you were superbly urbane, and I am sure big Arthur would have been proud of you. I would like to book you for mine – work permitting. I would like to be cremated. My favourite song is 'Smoke Gets in Your Eyes'. Okay that's fate. I will pay you when I see you down there.
>
> Love Eric
>
> PS Nothing in this letter constitutes a contract.

Ernie's moving contribution to the service was to read out the words to 'Bring Me Sunshine'. After a private cremation service at Garston, Eric's ashes were later returned to the church for burial in the Garden of Remembrance.

On 26 July 1984, BBC Radio 2 broadcast a tribute to Eric. At the start, Eric's widow, Joan, expressed her gratitude for the love the public had shown the family following the comedian's death. 'I have received thousands of letters, and my family and myself have read them all,' said Joan. 'And I have to say they've been an enormous comfort. I've been overwhelmed at the reaction of everybody that they should feel such grief for someone who isn't really a member of their family. And yet they all felt that he was.' The radio tribute was introduced by Roy Castle. He explained to the listeners that Eric introduced him to his then future wife, Fiona Dickson.

Eddie Braben shared a particularly touching tribute during the radio programme. 'The trouble is, when you go in search of perfection you very rarely find it,' he said. 'Eric Morecambe came as close as anyone. This constant striving for perfection brought with it that now familiar word "pressure". And this is where the most valuable person in his life deserves her tribute: his wife, Joan. It couldn't have been easy living with Eric when he was carrying the worries of his work. It must have been a great strain. But Joan never let it show. She is quite a remarkable lady. A lady of great charm, dignity and elegance, which never left her even when the going was severe. I honestly believe because of this wonderful lady we got a few extra years of Eric Morecambe magic that we weren't really entitled to.'

Charles Wallace had kept in mind his plans to shoot further scenes for *The Passionate Pilgrim* at Hever Castle in 1984. Morecambe's death meant these scenes were sadly never shot, but the film was released at cinemas in its original shorter form. Cable television broadcasts and VHS and DVD releases have also followed.

Thames Television recorded *Bring Me Sunshine* at The London Palladium on 9 November 1984. This tribute show was staged in memory of Eric and to raise much-needed funds for the British Heart Foundation. The evening was hosted by Ernie Wise, and the guests of honour were Joan Morecambe and the Duke of Edinburgh. The production was directed by Mark Stuart and produced by Philip Jones and Louis Benjamin. Meanwhile, Morecambe and Wise's agent Billy Marsh acted as a consultant to the programme. The show was broadcast on the ITV network on Christmas Day 1984 from 6.00pm until 8.30pm. The cast featured Michael Aspel, Kenny Ball and his Jazzmen, Alison Bell, Lionel Blair, Max Bygraves, Tommy Cannon and Bobby Ball, James Casey, Roy Castle, Petula Clark, Leslie Crowther, Barry Cryer, Suzanne Danielle, Jim Davidson, Dickie Davies, Frank

Finlay, Bruce Forsyth, Jill Gascoine, Cherry Gillespie, Hannah Gordon, the Half Wits, Susan Hampshire, Dickie Henderson, Benny Hill, Diane Keen, Bonnie Langford, Lulu, Francis Matthews, Fulton Mackay, Nanette Newman, Des O'Connor, Mick Oliver, Elaine Paige, Michael Parkinson, Bertice Reading, Angela Rippon, Wayne Sleep, Jimmy Tarbuck, John Thaw, the Tiller Girls, Arthur Tolcher, Bryn Williams, Eli Woods, Mike Yarwood, the Irving Davies Dancers and the Stephen Hill Singers.

The gala tribute brought an end to a very difficult year. Eric's family were obviously still coming to terms with life without him. In addition to mourning the loss of his lifelong friend and comedy partner, Ernie was now facing life as a solo performer again. The public too mourned for the loss of a performer they had come to know, love and welcome into their homes thanks to the mediums of radio and television.

11

A Legacy of
Laughter

O N 1 JANUARY 1985, ERNIE was booked to make the first official mobile phone call in the UK; just two days later, *Night Train to Murder* was finally broadcast on ITV. Ernie decided to tour Australia that year with his one-man show. However, sadness somewhat overshadowed this venture due to the death of his mother, Connie, at the age of eighty-five.

On a happier note, Ernie realised an ambition to appear in a sitcom in 1985 when he made a special guest appearance on the American series *Too Close for Comfort*. The series was based on the Thames Television sitcom *Keep it in the Family*, created by Brian Cooke. Wise's episode was called 'The British are Coming, the British are Coming'. Appropriately, he played a character called Ernie, a long-time friend of the lead character, Henry Rush, played by Ted Knight. Despite being married, Ernie goes on a blind date arranged by Rush. Inevitably, Ernie's wife turns up causing chaos for all involved.

Eric's wife, Joan, had her first book published on 11 November 1985. Entitled *Morecambe and Wife*, the book was very much a personal account of her life with Eric and their children.

After Eric had died, his son, Gary, discovered the comedian had been working on a new adult novel called *Stella*. A further search resulted in him finding approximately two thirds of the manuscript. With his mother's blessing, Gary went on to complete the novel. The book tells the story of a struggling entertainer from Lancashire called Stella Ravencroft who becomes a national star. First published in 1986, it's obvious that Eric had drawn from his own life for inspiration while writing the novel.

Gary himself has continued to be a highly successful author. The Morecambe-and-Wise-related books he has written or co-written include *Funny Man: Eric Morecambe*, *Morecambe and Wise: Behind the Sunshine*, *The Illustrated Morecambe*, *Memories of Eric*, *Eric*

Morecambe: Life's Not Hollywood It's Cricklewood, Eric Morecambe Unseen: The Lost Diaries, Jokes and Photographs, You'll Miss Me When I'm Gone: The Life and Work of Eric Morecambe, Eric Morecambe: Lost and Found, The Morecambe and Wise Story and *Morecambe and Wise: 50 Years of Sunshine*.

In February 1987, Ernie was reunited with Michael Aspel and Glenda Jackson when he appeared on Michael's LWT chat show, *Aspel and Company*. Also appearing on the same show was guest Gary Wilmot. The year also saw Ernie return to the stage to play the role of William Cartwright in *The Mystery of Edwin Drood*. This production was staged at the Savoy Theatre in London's West End. The Scottish actress and singer Lulu, who guested on *The Morecambe and Wise Show*, co-starred alongside Wise. The cast also included Julia Hills and Sarah Payne.

'When I was sent the script, I was knocked out,' Ernie explained in his autobiography. 'I listened to the score and thought how wonderful it was.' Ernie and the cast worked hard to make the show work. Sadly, it closed after just a ten-week run.

Ernie was back on the West End stage again only a few months later when he appeared in the hit Ray Cooney farce *Run for Your Wife*. Ernie took over the role of Detective Sgt Porterhouse from Eric Sykes. At the time, the long-running comedy was based at the

Criterion Theatre and starred Patrick Mower, John Quayle, Aimi Macdonald, Ron Aldridge, Leslie Lawton, John Hughes and Una Stubbs. Patrick and Una had, of course, made separate guest appearances on shows made by Morecambe and Wise at Thames.

In 1989, Ernie helped to raise funds for the heart charity CORDA by flying around the world in eighty hours dressed as Phileas Fogg. Marty Christian of The New Seekers accompanied Wise as his manservant.

In the same year, Ernie accepted an invitation to appear on an edition of *Rainbow*. Created by Pamela Lonsdale, the popular children's programme was made by Thames from 1972 to 1992. Even now, the programme and its catchy theme song are remembered with great affection. From 1974 until 1992, Geoffrey Hayes attempted to keep order over the characters of Zippy, George and Bungle in the *Rainbow* house. 'I remember we were all excited to have Ernie on the programme,' said series puppeteer, Ronnie Le Drew. 'We met him at our rehearsal room, which was in Teddington Yacht Club. He was very friendly, and Roy Skelton, who voiced Zippy and George, was thrilled to work with him. If I remember correctly, Roy had written the script. The premise was that Zippy dreamt he was being given a lesson by Ernie in how to tell a joke properly. Before we recorded the show, we all had lunch in the executive lounge, which was normally only used for executives at

Thames. Of course, the programme went without a hitch. We all agreed how nice it was to have such a nice man as a guest on *Rainbow*.'

Channel 4's letters-and-numbers game *Countdown* was the first programme to be broadcast on the channel when it started on 2 November 1982. By the end of the decade, then hosts Richard Whiteley and Carol Vorderman had become a hit with the series' viewers. Ernie was asked to guest in 'Dictionary Corner' and appeared in twelve editions of the show in all, travelling to Yorkshire Television's studios on Kirkstall Road in Leeds for the recordings. The programmes were broadcast between 18 and 25 January 1990 and between 22 and 29 August the same year.

Dedicated to his late comedy partner, Ernie's autobiography, *Still on My Way to Hollywood*, was first published on 20 September 1990. The following month, Ernie travelled to Thames Television's studios in Teddington on Halloween believing he was going to be interviewed about his new autobiography. Instead, he was presented with the 'big red book' by Michael Aspel and became the latest subject of *This is Your Life*.

Each edition of the programme had a code word used internally by the production team to keep the identity of the subject a secret. On this occasion, the code word was 'joining' – as in 'Can't see the join!' The guests appearing on the show were Johnny Ammonds,

Richard Baker, Michael Barratt, Jack Bentley, Lionel Blair, Eddie Braben, Annie Bradley (Ernie's sister), George Chisholm, Marty Christian, Jilly Cooper, Gemma Craven, Peter Cushing, Robin Day, Sid Green, Dick Hills, Edmund Hockridge, Jackie Hockridge, Laurie Holloway, Glenda Jackson, Philip Jenkinson, Philip Jones, David Lodge, Marion Montgomery, Joan Morecambe, Angela Rippon, Dorothy Ward, June Whitfield, Richard Whitmore, Doreen Wise, Gordon Wiseman (Ernie's brother) and Peter Woods. A letter was sent by Gene Kelly, and there were filmed tributes from Shirley Bassey, Pearl Carr and Teddy Johnson, Constance Dawson (Ernie's other sister) and Des O'Connor. The programme was broadcast on ITV on Wednesday 26 December 1990 at 6.45pm. Interestingly, during Eric's life Thames had made two approaches to the Morecambe family in the hope of presenting him with the 'big red book'. However, Eric had always made it clear that he didn't want to be the subject of the programme.

In July 1991, Ernie briefly appeared on the chat show *Wogan*. This edition was the last-ever programme to be broadcast by the corporation from the BBC Television Theatre in Shepherd's Bush prior to its sale. In a pre-recorded segment, Ernie recalled how he and Eric had made their first television series, *Running Wild*, at the theatre.

Ernie, Eddie Braben and Ernest Maxin were asked to appear in a new set of videos released by Watershed Pictures in 1991. In between a compilation of sketches from the BBC editions of *The Morecambe and Wise Show*, the men reminisced with affection about the days of working on the series.

In April 1992, Ernie paid a moving tribute on radio to Benny Hill, who passed away on Saturday 20 April 1992 during the Easter weekend. It was no secret that Hill and Morecambe and Wise were great admirers of each other's work.

Christmas that year saw Ernie playing the role of King in the pantomime *Sleeping Beauty* at the Theatre Royal, Windsor. The twice-daily show, which also starred Bryan Burdon, ran from 18 December 1992 to 23 January 1993. A rare video of an eight-minute sequence from the production was originally uploaded to YouTube in 2009. Set in a bedroom, it seems strange to watch Ernie playing a bed scene with another performer. Due to ill health, it would turn out to be Wise's last-ever pantomime.

Wise was the subject of a BBC documentary entitled *The Importance of Being Ernie*. Originally shown on 23 April 1993, the programme featured Ernie looking back on his life and career. It was not an enjoyable experience for Wise, and he was not happy with the way it portrayed him. He later told a fan, 'I fell out with the director. In the end it was just a put-down.' Following the upset caused by the documentary, Ernie withdrew more and more from public life. He spent more time with Doreen and his friends at his homes in Maidenhead and Florida. Ernie also suffered the first of his strokes during 1993. Later, after a second stroke, Wise reluctantly decided to sell his car and give up driving.

The BBC broadcast the first of three high-rating editions of a documentary series called *Bring Me Sunshine* starting on 14 May 1994. The short series was hosted by self-proclaimed Morecambe and Wise fan, Ben Elton. Those taking part and sharing their memories and thoughts on Eric and Ernie included Roy Castle, Fry and Laurie, Hale and Pace, Diana Rigg, and John Thaw. Ernie was unable to appear due to ill health.

With Morecambe and Wise very much in people's minds again in 1994, Paul McCartney confirmed in an interview that *The Morecambe and Wise Show (Two of a Kind)* was his favourite of all the television shows he had ever appeared on.

On 14 May 1995, Comic Heritage unveiled a plaque at 85, Torrington Park, London, the house Eric lived in from 1956 to 1961. Then, just months later, Ernie Wise announced his retirement from show business on 27 November 1995 – his seventieth birthday.

Dick Hills passed away on 6 June 1996. Hills and Green had continued working together; for instance, they wrote and adapted material for Cannon and Ball's television shows in the 1980s.

Ernie's last-ever television appearance was on *Auntie's All Time Greats*. Broadcast on 3 November 1996, the programme marked sixty years of BBC Television. Michael Parkinson hosted a star-studded gala from BBC Television Centre and presented awards to the shows and performers voted by viewers as their all-time favourites. Ernie and Eric's wife, Joan, both collected awards for 'Favourite Light Entertainment Series' and 'Best Light Entertainment Performers'.

Comic Heritage unveiled another plaque in honour of the tall one with the glasses on 11 May 1997. It was erected on a wall at the front of Teddington Studios. This, of course, was where Morecambe and Wise taped their shows for Thames Television.

Christmas 1998 saw BBC One broadcast a documentary called *Bring Me Sunshine – The Heart and Soul of Eric Morecambe*. Made by Watchmaker Productions as part of the *Omnibus* strand, the programme was a celebration of Eric's life and career. Again, due to his poor health, Ernie was unable to appear. Those taking part included Joan Morecambe, Gail Morecambe and Gary Morecambe, together with Johnny Ammonds, Dave Allen, Eddie Braben, Walter Butterworth, Bill Cotton, Dickie Davies, Mike Fountain, Michael Grade, Glenda Jackson and Des O'Connor. It arguably remains one of the very best documentaries made about the comedian to date.

Ernie suffered a heart attack while at his holiday home near Fort Lauderdale in Florida at the end of 1998. He had recently been on a cruise with Doreen and a group of his friends to celebrate his seventy-third birthday. Although he was taken to hospital, he was released by doctors not long afterwards. Sadly, Ernie suffered a more severe heart attack four days later and spent three weeks in intensive care. He then underwent a triple heart bypass.

At that stage, Doreen didn't believe Ernie was going to make it through the Christmas period. Ernie, though, was homesick and wanted to return to England. Since it would not be possible for him to travel on a commercial flight when he was so unwell, Doreen arranged for two doctors and a nurse to accompany them on a private flight in a Linear jet. The plane stopped twice to refuel, before finally landing at Northolt in north London. From there, an ambulance conveyed Wise to Nuffield Hospital near Slough. During the ambulance journey, Doreen told him, 'You're back now, you're home.'

Sadly, on 15 March 1999, it was announced that Sid Green had died. But the same month was to bring more bad news. Doctors had told Doreen that Ernie would be allowed to return to his Maidenhead home for a couple of hours on 21 March. 'We were going to have tea together, sitting in the garden,' Doreen said. 'He was so looking forward to it. It meant so much to him. He couldn't talk about anything else.' Unfortunately, Ernie suffered a third heart attack that morning. 'I went to the hospital, but he had already died from heart failure and complications following the operation, and he had had a chest infection,' said Doreen.

Ernie was aged seventy-three when he passed away. Johnny Ammonds, Michael Barratt, Frank Bough, Bill Cotton, Michael Grade, Laurie Holloway, David Lodge, Gail Morecambe, Gary Morecambe, Joan Morecambe, Tom O'Connor, Angela Rippon and Bert Weedon were among the mourners who attended the funeral service at Slough Crematorium on 30 March 1999.

Michael Grade read the eulogy. During the service he said, 'There is a sadness across the whole nation as we all have to say our last farewell to Ernie Wise, the last half of a beloved institution: the Morecambe and Wise comedy legend. He has managed to leave an indelible mark on the rich cultural history of his country. In the process, he found a place in the affections of millions of its inhabitants through his professional achievements.' Grade also added, 'Why were Morecambe and Wise more successful at making the whole nation laugh than anyone before or since? I think the answer is rather simple: there was Eric and Ernie and when you mix the two, they created a comedic chemistry that can only be explained in my view as something of a divine process, that really defies analysis.

'The written tributes of the past week have gone some way to redress a rather unfair imbalance in the appreciation of the genius of Morecambe and Wise which has tended to concentrate more on Eric's contribution and not enough on Ernie's. Let us be clear: they were equal partners in the comic genius department.'

Ernie's ashes were scattered during a small ceremony attended by Doreen and close friends on the riverbank close to his home. Doreen felt this was the perfect location after discovering an interview in which Wise said the riverbank was his favourite place in the world.

Eric and Ernie were each awarded a posthumous BAFTA fellowship in 1999. The emotional year also saw Graham Ibbeson's statue of Eric Morecambe unveiled on the seafront in Morecambe, Lancashire, by the Queen on 23 July. Aptly, the unveiling of the statue was accompanied by the playing of the song, 'Bring Me Sunshine'. Morecambe and Wise were also honoured with a plaque in 1999 to commemorate the three films they made for Rank at Pinewood Studios.

The tribute stage show *The Play What I Wrote* debuted on 27 September 2001 at the Liverpool Playhouse. The show was produced by David Pugh and directed by the well-known actor and film director Kenneth Branagh. The production was later staged at

Wyndham's Theatre in London's West End. The following year it gained two Olivier awards before crossing the Atlantic to New York in 2003. There it played with critical success on Broadway and was shortlisted for a Tony award.

ITV first broadcast the sixty-minute documentary *The Unforgettable Eric Morecambe* during November 2001. Narrated by Daniel Abineri, the programme included contributions from Joan Morecambe, Gail Morecambe and Gary Morecambe, together with Johnny Ammonds, Eddie Braben, Ronnie Corbett, Barry Cryer, Bill Drysdale, Mike Fountain, André Previn, Ann Hamilton, Ernest Maxin and Des O'Connor.

Later that decade, Eddie Braben's autobiography, *The Book What I Wrote*, was published in 2004. Braben peppered his story with wonderful anecdotes about the original straight man and his amiable sidekick.

Jimmy Tarbuck's daughter, Liza Tarbuck, narrated a new documentary called *Morecambe and Wise: The Greatest Moment* in 2007. First transmitted by UK Gold (now called GOLD), the programme featured a count-down of favourite moments chosen by viewers, and culminated in the showing of the most popular moment. Along the way, there were contributions from Joan Morecambe and Doreen Wise and several of Eric and Ernie's guests. They included Eddie Braben, Barry Cryer, Bruce Forsyth, Hannah Gordon, Ann Hamilton, Elton

John, Cliff Richard and Edward Woodward. Finally, it was revealed that viewers had voted 'The Stripper' sketch as Morecambe and Wise's 'greatest moment'.

New Year's Day 2008 saw BBC One broadcast a documentary called *Morecambe and Wise: In Their Own Words.* Introduced and narrated by Jonathan Ross, the programme focused on the double act's rise to the top, featuring clips to tell their story. Impressionist Jon Culshaw was also on hand to read a selection of transcripts of correspondence from the BBC's archives.

In January 2009, BBC One broadcast *Morecambe and Wise: The Show What Paul Merton Did.* In the programme, Merton celebrated the magic and genius of Eric and Ernie with the help of Eddie Braben, Jack Dee, Bruce Forsyth, Eddie Izzard, André Previn and Angela Rippon.

The year 2009 marked the twenty-fifth anniversary of Eric's untimely death and the tenth anniversary of Ernie's death. It was also the year that Bob Golding launched his award-winning one-man show, in which he played Eric Morecambe, at the famous Edinburgh Festival. The production also had a Christmas run at the Duchess Theatre in London's West End, following an extensive tour.

Victoria Wood developed and filmed a new BBC drama called *Ernie and Ernie* for transmission as part of the BBC's Christmas schedule in 2010. Victoria, who sadly died in 2016, played the role of Eric's mother, Sadie Bartholomew. 'I think we all have an image in our collective memory of Morecambe and Wise as two middle-aged men, with their backs to us, skipping,' she said in 2011. 'And probably lots of us can quote from the Mr Preview sketch with André Previn, and many of us may be unable to disassociate the music of "The Stripper" from Ernie having a go at some grapefruits.

'But they didn't emerge fully fledged as Britain's best-loved double act; they travelled a long road to arrive at that position. And it was that journey that interested me, particularly their early days in variety. Eric and Ernie met as teenagers – Ernie the polished child star, and Eric the rather more reluctant embryo comedian. I had thought for years that it was a story that needed to be told and I am so delighted that we were able to bring it to the screen.

'There is such a fondness for Morecambe and Wise, but I wanted us to tell a story that would mean something even more to an audience who had never heard of them. And Peter Bowker wrote a lovely heart-warming script that focused on their friendship, that bond that enabled them to weather the flop of their first television series, *Running Wild*, in 1954.

'I was one of millions who loved Morecambe and Wise, and our drama was a way of celebrating their talent, their history and their endearing friendship.'

Although Wood had considered the idea of making a follow-up film to dramatise the next part of the Morecambe and Wise story, this did not go beyond the initial conception stage.

Ernie's wife, Doreen, officially unveiled a statue of Wise in Morley, Leeds, where he once won a talent contest, in March 2010. Carved by sculptor Melanie Wilks, the statue depicted the performer with a furled umbrella and a straw boater, in reference to Morecambe's and Wise's famous 'Singin' in the Rain' routine. The statue was commissioned by the Morley Murals Committee with funding donated by Ernie's widow.

Miranda Hart's sitcom *Miranda* began on BBC One in 2009. The series was developed from her BBC Radio 2 comedy, *Miranda Hart's Joke Shop*. Although she had been climbing the comedy ladder for some time, this television series really cemented Hart in the public's consciousness. This fact, together with her admission that Eric was her 'hero' and 'inspiration', had not gone unnoticed by Eric's wife, Joan, and son, Gary. 'In Eric Morecambe I felt I found a friend with whom to share my life,' Miranda explained. 'Such was the immediacy of his humour and the warmth of his on-screen persona that I would put on a Morecambe and Wise video on a gloomy day, a day when the Black Dog might have been prowling, and the show would gently wash over me, lifting my mood. He would help me escape from how I was feeling, relieve the darkness. It wasn't just in bad times. I would laugh at him as I was laughing about positive things in my life, thereby sharing joyful moments with my beloved comedian too. He was there for me. I am not sure there are many comedians who are that open, endearing and approachable in their work to have such an effect on audiences. He was simply – unique.'

Such a fan of Morecambe's was Miranda that she included regular glances to camera, à la Eric in *The Morecambe and Wise Show*, in episodes of her sitcom. When she announced to BBC executives at a meeting that she wanted to do this, they seemed somewhat taken aback. While they might have been initially unconvinced by the idea, this device would go on to prove equally effective for Hart as it was for Eric. So too was her idea to employ the 'You have been watching...' caption, used so famously by David Croft at the close of his sitcoms, including *Dad's Army* and *Hi-de-Hi!*, at the end of each episode of *Miranda*.

Miranda was invited to visit Eric's wife, Joan, and son, Gary, at the Morecambe family home in May 2011. She jumped at the chance. Just two days before her visit to Harpenden, Miranda took part in a programme Ronnie Corbett was making about comedians and the performers who had inspired them. Corbett and his team asked Miranda to choose an iconic place related to her comedy hero as a filming location. Without hesitation, she said Fairfield Halls in Croydon where Eric and Ernie's live show was filmed in 1973. Having arrived at Fairfield Halls, Ronnie, on camera, showed Miranda around the venue. The programme also gave her an opportunity to stand on the venue's stage and perform her own version of the famous skip-dance.

In August 2011, new impressive waxworks of Eric and Ernie, which cost one hundred and fifty thousand pounds each to make, were unveiled by Joan Morecambe and Doreen Wise at Madame Tussauds' Blackpool home in 2011. Then, just a couple of months later, Ken Dodd unveiled the 'Comedy Carpet' on Blackpool's promenade. Made of granite and concrete, the four-million-pound installation took five years from conception to installation. In addition to their catchphrases including 'You can't see the join!', 'Not now, Arthur!', 'This boy's a fool!' and 'Tea, Ern?', the 'carpet' included memorable quotes and dialogue from some of Morecambe and Wise's television sketches, together with the lyrics to 'Bring Me Sunshine'.

December 2011 saw ITV's first transmission of *The Unforgettable Ernie Wise*. Those offering analysis during the tribute included Doreen Wise, together with Johnny Ammonds, Michael Barratt, Eddie Braben, Pearl Carr, Barry Cryer, Michael Grade, Ann Hamilton,

Laurie Holloway, Ernest Maxin, Joan Morecambe and Teddy Johnson.

It was the turn of television channel GOLD to celebrate the legendary Morecambe and Wise in 2012. Beginning on 21 November, viewers were treated to a five-part documentary series narrated by Victoria Wood called *Bring Me Morecambe and Wise*. The themes covered included Eric and Ernie's sketches, plays, guests and Christmas specials. Eric's wife, Joan, was on hand to give her unique insight into her husband and Ernie. There were also views from the comedy pair's admirers including Hugh Dennis, Stephen Mangan and Chris Tarrant.

In 2013, we lost two men who contributed hugely to the long and successful careers of Morecambe and Wise. On 13 February, Johnny Ammonds, who started with the duo back on their radio series *YoYo (You're Only Young Once)* and later produced and directed many of the BBC and Thames TV shows, died aged eighty-eight. Then, just over three months later, it was announced on 21 May that Eddie Braben, often cited as the third member of Morecambe and Wise, had sadly passed away aged eighty-two. Shortly after his death, *Eddie Braben's Morecambe and Wise Book* was published.

Miranda Hart was able to indulge her passion for Eric Morecambe again when she presented *My Hero: Miranda Hart on Eric Morecambe*. The programme was originally broadcast by BBC One on 29 March 2013. Narrated by Lesley Manville, the programme included new interviews with Eddie Braben, Barry Cryer, Dickie Davies, Ann Hamilton and Nick Owen.

A blue plaque was unveiled as a tribute to both Morecambe and Wise at Teddington Studios on 19 May 2013. The plaque was unveiled by Eric's wife, Joan, and daughter, Gail, in front of guests including Michael Aspel, Bernard Cribbins, Liz Fraser, Ernest Maxin, Jacki Piper, Su Pollard and Angela Rippon.

Following a sell-out run at the Edinburgh Fringe in 2013, and a hugely successful tour, the play *Eric and Little Ern*, written and performed by Ian Ashpitel and Jonty Stephens, was staged at the Vaudeville Theatre in London's West End during Christmas 2013. The production received rave reviews and standing ovations in the process. Eric's son, Gary, saw the show and loved it. He met the boys afterwards, and the two men are now firm friends with the Morecambe family. At the time of writing, *Eric and Little Ern* continues to tour the country and has recently played two dates at the Duke of York's Theatre in the West End.

On Christmas Day 2013, *Morecambe and Wise: In Pieces* began its first run on BBC Two. Presented by Penelope Keith, each of the five sixty-minute editions featured highlights from Eric and Ernie's BBC programmes. The guests in the clips included Peter

Cushing, Glenda Jackson, André Previn and June Whitfield.

Police were called to the site of Eric's statue in Morecambe on 11 October 2014 following reports that the statue had been damaged. A man, who was subsequently arrested and detained under the Mental Health Act, had tried to saw off one of the legs on the statue. Graham Ibbeson, who designed the sculpture, repaired the statue with the assistance of a London foundry, and the statue was back on display in the December of 2014. Eric's daughter, Gail, told the media the family felt 'moved' that the people of Morecambe 'cared so much' about the statue.

In April 2015, Joan Morecambe received an OBE from Her Majesty the Queen at Windsor Castle. Joan, who was accompanied at the ceremony by Gail, Gary and Steven, received the award for work with children's charities. At the time she was raising funds for Save the Children and was a patron of the A-T Society, which helps young people with a progressive genetic condition called Ataxia-Telangiectasia. Ever modest, Joan forgot to mention who her famous husband was, giving her second name as Bartholomew instead of Morecambe. By the time the fact came up in conversation, the press had left.

On what would have been Eric's ninetieth birthday on 14 May 2016, Lancaster City Museum opened an exhibition called *Bring Me Sunshine: The Legacy and*

Laughs of Eric Morecambe. It featured theatre and film posters, scripts, records and other items relating to Eric and his Morecambe and Wise days.

The first ever statue depicting Eric Morecambe and Ernie Wise together was unveiled on 14 October 2016 at Blackpool's world-famous Winter Gardens. It was commissioned to commemorate seventy-five years since Eric and Ernie first made their debut as a double act. The eight-feet-tall bronzed statue, which cost seventy-five thousand pounds to make, was the work of sculptor Graham Ibbeson. The statue was unveiled by Eric's widow Joan, daughter Gail and son Gary. A representative for Ernie's wife, Doreen, was also present. The ceremony was attended by fans of the comedy duo and members of the media.

Channel 5 broadcast *The Morecambe and Wise Story: Look Back in Laughter* for the first time in 2016. This documentary, which didn't feature a narrator, told Eric and Ernie's story through archive interview footage and recollections from family and friends. Eric's children, Gail and Gary, featured in the programme. In addition, there were appearances from Michael Barratt, Tim Brooke-Taylor, Walter Butterworth, Barry Cryer, Michael Grade, Ann Hamilton, Anita Harris and Des O'Connor.

Miranda Hart made the switch to ITV to front a documentary on Morecambe and Wise when she presented *Miranda: Morecambe and Wise and Me*. The ninety-minute documentary was shown by ITV on New Year's Day 2017. Those sharing their memories and personal anecdotes of Eric and Ernie included Richard Ayoade, Warwick Davis, Sarah Hadland, Glenda Jackson, Paddy McGuinness, Des O'Connor, André Previn, Angela Rippon, Jonathan Ross, Jimmy Tarbuck and David Walliams.

In 2017, Eric's former car, a Jensen Interceptor, was sold for over ninety-five thousand pounds at auction. The car was found by Nick Whale in Belgium back in 2014. Having restored it to its former glory, Whale decided to let someone else have the pleasure of owning and driving the vehicle.

A two-part documentary called *Morecambe and Wise Forever* was broadcast by ITV during Easter 2017. Narrated by Martin Clunes, the programmes featured interviews with Joan Morecambe, Gail Morecambe, Gary Morecambe, Steven Morecambe and Doreen Wise. The other contributors included Fenella Fielding, Hannah Gordon, Michael Grade, Anita Harris, Suzanne Lloyd and Millicent Martin. Highlights of the documentary included footage of Eric's daughter, Gail, and son, Gary, visiting the house in Morecambe where their comedian father was born. Mike Fountain also chauffeured Gail and Gary through Morecambe in the Rolls Royce that Eric had owned; and there were emotional scenes when Gary and Walter Butterworth were reunited with the Jenson Interceptor that Walter drove when Eric was suffering his first heart attack in 1968.

On 29 December 2017, *Eric and Ernie's Home Movies* was shown on BBC Two for the very first time. The sixty-minute programme featured footage filmed in the 1950s and 1960s at home, on holiday and relaxing between work engagements. Joan Morecambe, Gail Morecambe, Gary Morecambe and Steven Morecambe all appeared to discuss the films. In addition, there were interviews with Fiona Castle, William Cook, Ken Dodd, Laurie Holloway and Ceri Stennett.

On the same evening, BBC Four premiered *Eric, Ernie and Me*. Written by Neil Forsyth, and made by Objective Fiction, the one-off, sixty-minute drama featured the story of Eddie Braben and his working relationship with Morecambe and Wise. Forsyth was inspired to pitch the idea to the BBC after reading Braben's memoir, *The Book What I Wrote*. *Drop the Dead Donkey*'s Stephen Tompkinson took on the role of Eddie Braben, and Mark Bonnar and Neil Maskell played Eric and Ernie respectively. The cast also included Liz White, who played Braben's wife, Dee. Meanwhile, the production was directed by Dan Zeff.

After a five-year battle with ill health, Ernie's wife, Doreen, sadly passed away on 14 April 2018 aged eighty-six. Later that year, Ernest Maxin died on 27 September at the remarkable age of ninety-five.

Teddington Studios, the one-time home of Thames Television, was closed at the end of 2014. The complex was later demolished and has since been replaced with a residential development. To ensure that the history of the site is never forgotten, the management of a nearby public house called The Anglers decided to erect a collection of plaques in 2019 that pay tribute to some of the performers who worked there. Amongst the plaques commemorating the likes of Tommy Cooper, Benny Hill, Irene Handl and Sidney James was one dedicated to both Eric Morecambe and Ernie Wise. This was an exact replica of the plaque that Joan Morecambe and Gail Morecambe unveiled at Teddington Studios in May 2013.

The landscape of British television comedy may have changed dramatically since Morecambe and Wise were making their shows, but it's interesting to note that many of their fans weren't even born when the duo were still together. This would surely have pleased Eric who once said to his daughter, 'Gail, when I'm gone, you will watch the videos? You will watch them? If you don't watch them, then it was all for nothing.'

Thanks to the latest technology, we can now listen to Morecambe and Wise's radio shows and recordings, and watch their programmes and films, whenever we like. Eric's wife, Joan, believes her husband would have embraced modern technology if he was alive today. 'I think Eric would have bought all the gimmicks going. I think he would have loved learning all about the internet as he used to buy every new contraption that came along. He would have loved it!'

Joan is understandably pleased about the ongoing interest in the double act. 'People still have tremendous nostalgia for Eric and Ernie. That real love has carried on right through.' People often ask what Eric would have done if Ernie had passed away first. Although Eric had considered slowing down towards the end of his life, Joan is convinced he wouldn't have retired immediately. 'Eric would have carried on the business for a while,' she explained. 'But he had reached the stage where he was happy to write and just do a few things. However, he never wanted to stay at the top until the public tired of him. He felt that you've got to know when to leave.'

November 2019 saw the start of a four-part retrospective on GOLD called *Trust Morecambe and Wise*. Hosted by Lenny Henry, the series was recorded in front of a live studio audience in TC1, one of three remaining studios at Television Centre. More importantly, it was one of the studios used by the duo when they taped their shows at the BBC from 1968 to 1977. Each programme included interviews with guests including

Eric's son, Gary, together with Michael Grade, Susan Hampshire, Glenda Jackson and Angela Rippon.

Double acts may have come and gone since Morecambe and Wise last worked together, but none has ever come close to replacing them. Asked if she agreed, Ann Hamilton replied, 'There has never been anyone as funny as them on television.' Eric's daughter, Gail, once summarised the duo in just one word: 'unique'. Their legacy is arguably the work they've left behind – work that will no doubt continue to bring new generations laughter for many years to come.

Sources

I N ADDITION TO THE author's own archive of research material, the following sources have been used during the process of writing and researching this publication:

Books

Eric Morecambe: Life's Not Hollywood, It's Cricklewood, Gary Morecambe (BBC Books)

Eric Morecambe: Lost and Found, Gary Morecambe and Paul Burton (Biteback Publishing)

Eric Morecambe On Fishing, Eric Morecambe (Pelham Books)

Little Ern!: The Authorised Biography of Ernie Wise, Robert Sellers and James Hogg (Sidgwick and Jackson)

Memories of Eric, Gary Morecambe and Martin
    Sterling (Andre Deutsch Ltd)
Morecambe and Wise, Graham McCann (Fourth Estate)
Morecambe and Wise: Behind the Sunshine, Gary
    Morecambe and Martin Sterling (Pan Books)
Morecambe and Wise: You Can't See the Join, Jeremy
    Norvick (Andre Deutsch Ltd)
Still on My Way to Hollywood, Ernie Wise with Trevor
    Barnes (Gerald Duckworth and Co Ltd)

Newspapers

Blackpool Gazette
Daily Mirror
Dublin Evening Press
Evening Standard
The Stage
Yorkshire Evening Post

Magazines

Melody Maker
Studio News, Thames Television's in-house magazine
TV Mirror

DVDs

*From Headlines to 'Tight-Lines': The Story of ATV
    Today* (MACE)
Morecambe and Wise: Complete BBC Collection
    (2entertain)

Morecambe and Wise – Movie Collection (ITV Studios)
The Morecambe and Wise Show – The Thames Years (Network)
Morecambe and Wise – Two of a Kind: The Complete Series (Network)

Websites

BBC – www.bbc.co.uk
BBC Genome Project – genome.ch.bbc.co.uk
Morecambe and Wise – Paul Jenkinson and Gideon Chilton's website dedicated to Eric Morecambe and Ernie Wise: www.morecambeandwise.com